ENJOY THE BEAUTY
OF THE NAVAL ACADEMY!

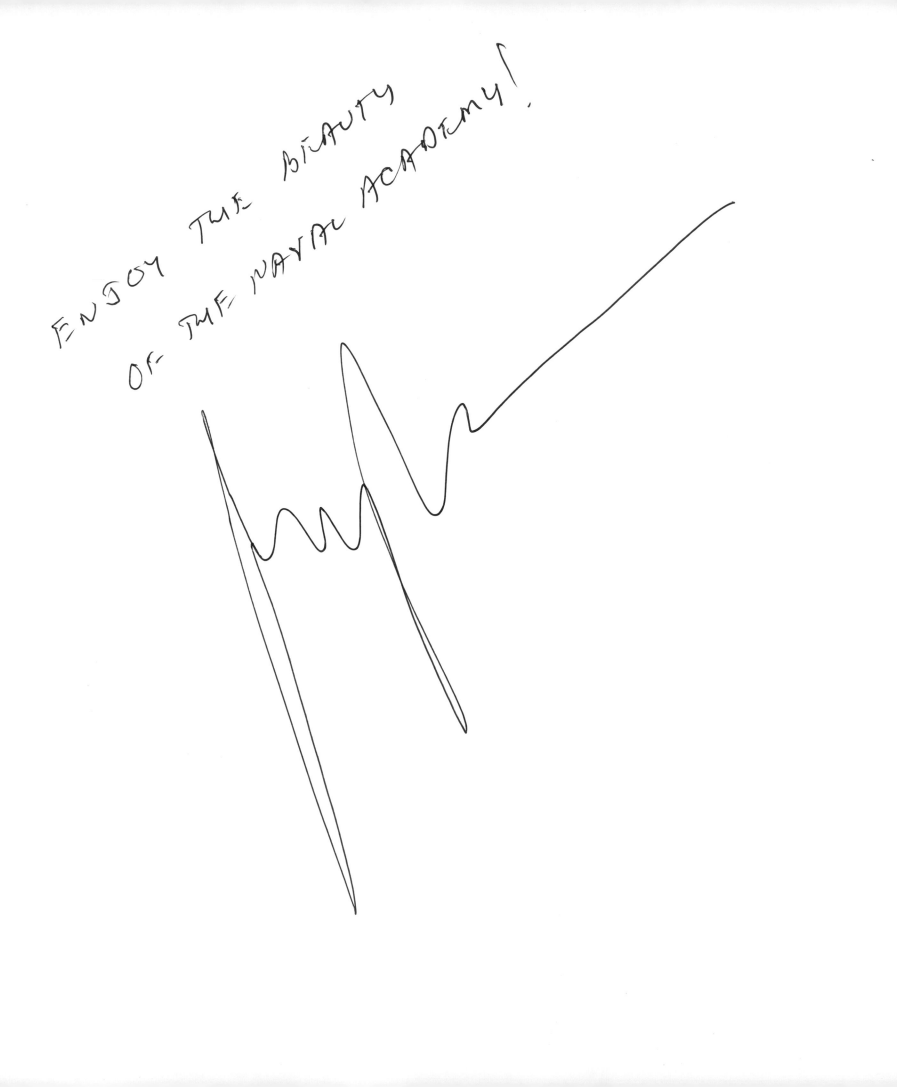

NAVAL ACADEMY
ANNAPOLIS

WRITING BY
GINNY PEARCE

FOREWORD BY
PRESIDENT JIMMY CARTER

PHOTOGRAPHY BY
ROGER MILLER

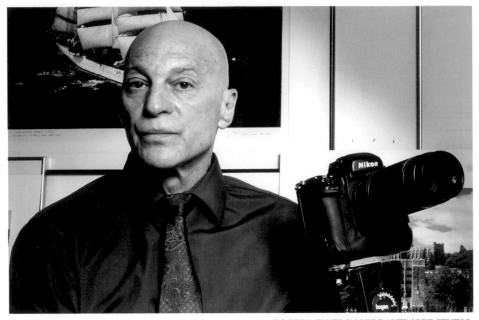

ROGER MILLER IN HIS BALTIMORE STUDIO

image publishing, ltd.
1411 Hollins Street / Union Square
Baltimore, MD 21223-2417
(tel) 410_566_1222   (cell) 410_245_2395   (fax) 410_233_1241
(email) roger.miller44@verizon.net   rcm.ipl44@gmail.com
(web) rogermillerphoto.net

DEDICATION
TO CHARLES JOHN EDWARD MILLER
I would like to dedicate this book to my dad, the most honorable sailor in my life. He was truly the "citizen" sailor and even though he never liked guns or fighting, he served his country in its time of need. He was the Chief Motor Machinist Mate First-Class on LST-55 and was in Operation Tiger and D-Day Invasion at Omaha Beach, and made 50 additional crossings of the English Channel. He loved the Navy, he loved his country and he loved his family. Thanks Dad, we miss you!

ROGER MILLER, 07-15-15

SPECIAL THANKS
A very special thanks to **THE HONORABLE JIMMY CARTER** for writing a very touching forward to this book and allowing me to meet him and take his portrait at the Carter Center in Atlanta, Georgia.

A very special thanks to **CAPTAIN ROGER E. TETRAULT**, '63 USN (Ret); **REAR ADMIRAL WILLIAM C. MILLER**, '62; USN (Ret); **DANIEL "DAN" AKERSON**, '70; **GENERAL PETER PACE**, '67 US Marine Corps (Ret) all of these Distinguished Graduates for writing very informative and personal accounts of what the Naval Academy has meant to their lives and careers. Thank you to the **NAVAL ACADEMY ALUMNI ASSOCIATION** and the **NAVAL ACADEMY FOUNDATION** for help with the distinguished graduates.

Thanks to **JEFFREY WOLK,** one of my best friends, partner and mentor, thanks you for all the training with Lightroom, Photoshop and InDesign. You have made my photography 500% better. We have also helped hundreds of people understand digital photography in the last couple of years. Onward and upward for both of us! Thanks to **ROBERT CLARK, CARRIE KIEWITT, JULIE WESTERN, JODY DALTON** and everybody at **HISTORIC ANNAPOLIS, Inc** for keeping Annapolis historically beautiful. We have done a lot to capture its beauty in the last couple of years. Thanks to the **BALTIMORE CAMERA CLUB** and all my friends and fellow photographers who have helped me refine and find my VISION. Thanks to **KEVIN MURPHY** who is my friend when I needed him and my chase boat captain in rough and calm seas. Thanks to **JACK REA** of **SERVICE PHOTO** for his expertise with my "baby" Nikons and all his help with digital photography.

ROGER MILLER, 07-15-15

INFORMATION
The inclusion of any entity, company or corporation in this book, is in no way to be construed as an endorsement of that entity, company or corporation by the United States Naval Academy, the United States Navy or the United States Marine Corps. Any inclusion in this book is solely by the editorial judgement of the publisher.

2

BRIGADE OFFICER WITH SWORD

SPECIAL THANKS
A very special thanks to everyone at the **UNITED STATES NAVAL ACADEMY** for allowing me access to all of their sites and activities during the last few years. I would especially like to thank the following people: **VICE ADMIRAL TED CARTER,** Superintendent and his wife for allowing me to photograph Buchanan House, **VICE ADMIRAL MIKE MILLER,** former Superintendent, and **VICE ADMIRAL JEFFREY L. FOWLER,** former Superintendent for allowing me to work on this book; **CAPTAIN BILL BYRNE,** Commandant of Midshipmen, for allowing me access to all of his midshipmen; **FREDERICK DAVIS, PhD,** Associate Dean for Academic Affairs, for his assistance in getting photos of the academic departments; **JIM CHEEVERS,** Head Curator of the U.S. Naval Museum and good friend, for reviewing the text for details and historic accuracy, and always having the correct answers; **MICHAEL E. BRADY,** Strategic Communications Director and good friend, for his support with this project; **DAVID HOFFBERGER,** Chapel Center Facilities Manager and good friend, for allowing me access to the chapels and for reviewing the text concerning the chapels; **JENNIFER ERICKSON,** Media Relations Director and most beautiful smile on the yard, for her day-to-day help on the book and **COLLEEN ROY KRUEGER,** Public Affairs Specialist and the second best smile on the yard, for being my escort of choice. **LEO S. MAHALIC** of the PAO for his help doing photographs and explaining sailing to me. **COMMANDER JOHN SCHOFIELD** PAO officer for his help. **ENSIGN ALEC BACON** for his help in editing. **ACADEMIC INSTRUCTORS** Thanks to the many academic instructors at the Academy – too many to mention by name – for all of you who let me photograph you in action and provided information about your departments. A special thanks to **CHRISTY STANLAKE,** my one and only favorite English professor, who puts on the plays every year with the **MASQUERADERS,** for letting me take photos of the plays. Thanks to **MONTY MAXWELL,** Chapel Organist at the USNA chapel, for his great music, the All Saints program and letting me photograph him at the organ. **USNA SPORTS** Thank you **CHUCK GLADCHUCK** for access to all the sports venues. A big thanks to **SCOTT STRASEMEIER** for putting up with scheduling me. Thanks to **JOE RUBINO** for all his advice and keeping everything going at the academy. Thank you to the midshipmen that helped me to photograph the uniforms: **CAMERON WOODS, MANSFIELD MURPH, KARA YINGLING, CHRISTOPHER SIMMONS, IVAN DYSANGCO, CAROLYNE VU** and **PETER DESCHLER.** A special thanks to **JUDY BUDDENSICK** and **JOHN VORNDICK** midshipmen sponsors for letting me do photographs of their homes.

ROGER MILLER, 07-15-15

CREDITS
Photography by **ROGER MILLER**
Design and Layout by **ROGER MILLER**
Foreword by **THE HONORABLE JIMMY CARTER**
Writing by **GINNY PEARCE**
Editing by **ROGER MILLER, GINNY PEARCE, JIM CHEEVERS, USNA PAO, and AMANDA HUNTER**

INFORMATION
Library of Congress Control Number: .
ISBN # 0-911897-63-1   ISBN # 9- 780-911897-63-0
Printed in China.

ORDERS
For direct orders please call or write for the specific pricing and the postage and handling to **IMAGE PUBLISHING, LTD**. at the above address. Discounts are available for stores, institutions and corporations, with minimum order requirements. You may also contact us for sales through our email. The suggested retail price at the time of publication is **US$39.95.**

STRIBLING WALK in front of **BANCROFT HALL** is a great place to visit in the spring when the garden is at its best. Midshipmen walk along Stribling Walk to get from their quarters in Bancroft Hall to their classrooms in one of the academic buildings.

THE UNITED STATES NAVAL ACADEMY COLOR GUARD is a group of specially-selected midshipmen who carry the colors as representatives of the U.S. Navy and the Naval Academy at all Naval Academy events and any public events for which they are requested.

TABLE OF CONTENTS

JIMMY CARTER - OUR NATION'S 39th PRESIDENT (1977-1981), Jimmy Carter, graduated from the United States Naval Academy in 1946 (class of '47). It is fitting that The Honorable Jimmy Carter would write the foreword to the *Naval Academy Annapolis*, as he not only graduated in the top ten percent of his USNA class, but he also served our country for seven years as a naval officer and for four years as President and Commander-in-Chief. Jimmy Carter is a perfect example of the Naval Academy's mission to develop leaders to serve the Nation, for his unparalleled accomplishments, in and out of office, in alleviating suffering and extending democracy and peace throughout the world.

FOREWORD
BY THE HONORABLE JIMMY CARTER

As a child, even at the age of five, my only ambition was to go to Annapolis and be a naval officer. This was during the Great Depression and, at the time, a motivation for my family was that the two military academies offered excellent educations without prohibitive costs. My family had been in America for 300 years, all were farmers, and neither my father nor any of his Carter ancestors had an opportunity to finish high school. Daddy, though, had completed the tenth grade at Riverside Military Academy, and was in a naval training program – on the Chattahoochee River! Also, my favorite uncle was a radioman on active duty in the Pacific fleet. As the lightweight boxing champion, he solidified my preference for service at sea.

Plebe year in my day was quite severe, to put it mildly, and I garnered more than my share of hazing - partly because as a southerner I refused to sing such obnoxious songs as "Marching Through Georgia." I became highly proficient though on the commando course, could easily do 94 pushups (twice 47), and set some speed records in changing uniforms inside a cruise box. In my spare time, on duty days, I was always eager to spend as many hours as possible as a passenger, and sometime pilot, in PBY and OS2U seaplanes.

Study time was highly focused for our class, which was almost the last of the wartime classes to complete four years of study in just three years. We finished in 1946 instead of 1947. On our 1944 training cruise in the Mediterranean, we either had an encounter with a reef or a German torpedo (we never knew which), and the old *U.S.S. New York* had one of its propeller blades torn off. We limped back to the Philadelphia Naval Yard for repairs - our only real contact with World War II.

I think it's accurate to say that we had mixed emotions when our naval heroes, including Admiral Chester Nimitz, came to the Academy to speak to us, especially after 1945. We were glad the war was over, grieved over a number of our first-classmen who were lost, and felt somewhat guilty that we had not been personally involved in combat.

No Naval Academy graduate had become president before our class, and we have all been honored that our classmates have included two medal of honor recipients, a chairman of the Joint Chiefs of Staff and Ambassador to the Court of St. James in London, a Rhodes scholar and head of the CIA, and many others who have equally distinguished themselves but without as much public recognition.

Like all other Academy midshipmen, we learned the rudiments of manhood and citizenship, still well expressed in my aging copy of *The Bluejacket's Manual*. We were "expected to exhibit obedience, knowledge, fighting spirit, reliability, loyalty, initiative, self-control, energy, courage, justice, faith in ourselves, honor and cheerfulness." But the overarching criterion was truth – absolute truth, which was described as "the final test of a man." These criteria are extremely demanding, and it's quite likely that we have all deviated from this standard of almost absolute perfection.

But that final test – truth – was deeply imbedded in the consciousness of us all, and it stood me in good stead during my 1976 presidential campaign. After the assassinations of the Kennedy brothers and Martin Luther King, Jr., revelations about the criminal activities of our CIA, and the false statements later revealed about Vietnam and Watergate, American voters responded to a simple promise never to be told a lie.

Rosalynn and I have relished the personal friendships made with Naval Academy classmates, and with shipmates from the *Wyoming*, *Mississippi*, *Pomfret*, *K-1*, and the *Sea Wolf*. One of the highlights of my career was to return to Annapolis as Commander-in-Chief, pardon all demerits having been earned by midshipmen, and give the graduation address. As I looked at the eager young faces, male and female, black and white, I was flooded with the realization that times change – often quite rapidly – but basic principles remain the same.

This wonderful book has brought back overwhelming memories, and helped me to relive exciting and gratifying years in the U.S. Navy. I am certain that everyone who has shared some of the same experiences will have the same feeling, and that many of our relatives and friends who absorb the text and photographs will feel a glow of goodwill and gratitude to those who have served our nation in this way.

Jimmy Carter

A NEW CLASS OF PLEBES line up in front of Bancroft Hall for a class photo. The plebes' day begins at 5:30 a.m. with calisthenics and a run. After their run, the Plebes go to morning meal formation and then to morning meal. The plebes have formations before every meal, during which attendance is taken and uniforms are inspected. Tourists are able to see these formations.

INTRODUCTION

More than a million visitors come to Annapolis each year for a guided tour of the United States Naval Academy, one of America's premiere four-year colleges, where many of our future Navy and Marine officers, known as midshipmen, receive four years of undergraduate academic and professional training. Visitors enjoy the natural beauty of the Academy with its historic buildings, monuments and museum that recall some of the country's naval history. Some visitors may also enjoy a sporting event, band concert or theatrical play. It is likely visitors will see some of the midshipmen in their uniforms as they hurry to and from classes or participate in a training exercise. And if you time your visit just right, you may see a formal parade of the entire Naval Academy Brigade of Midshipmen.

The photos in this book will take you on a tour of the academy and beyond. Its vast 338-acre campus blends in perfectly with the quaint historic seaport town of Annapolis which is also Maryland's State Capitol. Located at the confluence of the Severn River and the Chesapeake Bay, it is the perfect setting for training future naval officers. Enjoy photos that capture every part of the campus from the air, the land and on the water. The Academy is a National Historic Landmark as many of its magnificent buildings, such as the Naval Academy Chapel and Bancroft Hall, are more than a hundred years old. You will also see new facilities such as the Wesley Brown Field House, new soccer stadium, new Jewish Chapel, the newly-renovated Museum and more.

See inside buildings not opened to the public. Get a detailed look at the architecture, murals, plaques and other symbols of the past and present. Visit classrooms where our future officers receive state-of-the art academic training with a core curriculum and electives designed to prepare them for any career field in the Navy or Marine Corps. Get a glimpse of the many day-to-day activities in which the midshipmen are required to participate. Outside the walls of the Academy, this photographic tour will take you to various Naval and Marine Corps bases where midshipmen receive professional and leadership training. You will see men and women receiving hands-on training in operations as they participate in drills and mock battles, fly aboard Navy aircraft, plunge below the surface of the seas in nuclear submarines or cruise the world on Navy ships. The Department of Defense and the Department of the Navy invests their resources in this comprehensive training of these young men and women so that they will be effective officers in their assignments after graduation.

Encouraging a sense of pride and spirit, the mission of the Naval Academy is "To develop midshipmen morally, mentally and physically and to imbue them with the highest ideals of duty, honor and loyalty in order to graduate leaders who are dedicated to a career of naval service and have potential for future development in mind and character to assume the highest responsibilities of command, citizenship and government."

Each summer, more than 1,000 plebes, first-year midshipmen, arrive at the Naval Academy to learn to live up to this mission. See photos of the plebes as they face a summer that includes the strenuous physical training of boot camp and the discipline of military training which is part of the plebes' yearlong development system. It requires them to produce under pressure, to respond promptly and intelligently to orders, and to measure up to the highest standards of honor, courage and commitment.

In addition to rigorous training, plebes begin learning a whole new vocabulary of naval terms and the midshipmen seniority which is different from traditional colleges. All Naval Academy students, men and women, are called midshipmen, which is a rank between master chief (E-9) and the lowest grade of chief warrant office (W-2) in the Navy. Instead of being freshmen, sophomores, juniors and seniors, midshipmen are referred to as first, second, third or fourth class. A midshipman first class is a senior or "firstie." The student body is the Brigade of Midshipmen, or simply 'the Brigade.' The Brigade is divided into two regiments with three battalions each. Five companies make up each battalion, making a total of 30 companies.

The Brigade is headed by a first class midshipman, chosen for outstanding leadership performance, to be Brigade Commander. He or she is responsible for much of the Brigade's day-to-day activities, as well as the professional training of other midshipmen. Overseeing all Brigade activities is the Commandant of Midshipmen, an active-duty Navy Captain or Marine Corps Colonel. Working for the Commandant, experienced Navy and Marine Corps officers and senior enlisted leaders oversee each company.

The Naval Academy offers a demanding four-year program. Each graduate is awarded a Bachelor of Science degree in his or her chosen field of study and a commission as an Ensign in the Navy or as a Second Lieutenant in the Marine Corps. Each graduate serves his or her country with a minimum of five years as an officer.

In his quest to establish a formal Academy to train a "proper corps of sea officers," Captain John Paul Jones wrote in 1783, "in times of peace, it is necessary to prepare, and be always prepared for war by sea." The legacy of Captain Jones is reflected in both the grandeur of the Academy's landscape and in the exceptional men and women who bring it to life.

Inside the grand **ROTUNDA** entrance to **BANCROFT HALL**, high over the central door is a mural showing the battleship *USS SOUTH DAKOTA* in the Battle of Santa Cruz during World War II. It was painted by the Navy combat artist Commander Dwight C. Shepler. The sprawling dormitory complex is full of reminders of our proud naval heritage, including rooms dedicated to the Medal of Honor recipients who lived in them when they were themselves midshipmen.

HISTORY

Tracing its origins to the Continental Navy, established on October 13, 1775 with two vessels armed for combat against British merchant ships during the American Revolutionary War, the United States Navy of today is the world leader in naval readiness, employing state-of-the-art submarines, aircraft and ships.

In the 1800's, a naval officer's notoriety was based on his ability to maneuver his ship. Gunfire was incredibly inaccurate beyond 200 yards, so the success of warfare depended upon the naval officer's competence in maneuvering his ship close to the enemy and simultaneously summoning his fire-power upon the enemy ship, before the enemy had an opportunity to fire upon his vessel. These battles were fought upon "square-rigged" ships, good at catching the wind, but not easy to maneuver. The skill required to command with such accuracy and competence took a lifetime of practice and was left to the officers onboard to train and educate their successors.

Although a few schools were established to offer assistance in preparing midshipmen for their advancement examination (required after 1819), it was the practical "school of hard knocks" that really prepared them. Recognizing this disparity in 1825, President John Quincy Adams urged Congress to create a single Naval Academy "for the formation of scientific and accomplished officers."

In the 1830's, most midshipmen approaching examinations for promotion were assigned to a naval school in Philadelphia for eight months. The "Philadelphia Naval Asylum" was a poorly equipped, informal program, relying on retired sailors to share their years of experience with the young maritime students.

Fortunately, in 1842, Professor William Chauvenet began taking steps to improve the program while planning for a permanent Academy. That same year, the American Brig *Somers* set sail as a school ship for training teenage naval apprentice volunteers. Discipline deteriorated on the *Somers* and there was an attempted mutiny. The incident cast doubt over the wisdom of sending midshipmen directly aboard ship to learn by doing.

In 1845, the newly appointed Secretary of the Navy, historian George Bancroft, having given serious consideration to Chauvenet's proposal, established a national naval school at a 10-acre Army post named Fort Severn on the eastern tip of Annapolis, Maryland.

The school's first superintendent, Commander Franklin Buchanan, the faculty staff of seven and approximately 50 midshipmen attended the formal opening on October 10, 1845. It began as a five-year academic and professional program (with the first and last years spent at sea). The curriculum included mathematics and navigation, gunnery and steam, chemistry, natural philosophy, English and French. In 1850, the Naval School officially became known as the United States Naval Academy, and the educational program became the consecutive four-year course of study which was the basis for the advanced curriculum at the Naval Academy today with training at sea during summer cruises. The sloop *Preble* became the first practice ship assigned to the Academy.

As our country has evolved socially and technologically, so has the Academy. In 1865, a permanent Academy Marine detachment was created, and in 1882, Congress allowed for the commissioning of Academy graduates as Second Lieutenants in the United States Marine Corps.

In 1930, the Academy received is accreditation from the Association of American Universities, and in 1931 the first Bachelor of Science Degrees were awarded to all graduates. In 1949, Midshipman Wesley Brown made history as the first African-American graduate of the Naval Academy, setting the stage for continued positive growth in the years ahead.

The 1950's and 60's brought the Honor Concept into effect. SAT scores were used in place of the Academy's own admission exam. A new academic program was initiated allowing electives to be taken in addition to the fixed curriculum, and a majors program was added, essentially eliminating a preset curriculum. The Trident Scholar program was launched, and the positions of Dean of Admissions and civilian Academic Dean were created.

In the 1970's, the Academy mirrored our nation's progress in equal rights when the first female joined the faculty. The first female midshipmen were admitted in 1976, through an official act of Congress authorizing the admission of women into all of the service academies.

As the U.S. Navy grew over the years, the Academy expanded. The campus of 10 acres increased to 338. The original student body of 50 midshipmen grew to a brigade size of 4,000. Modern granite buildings have replaced the old wooden structures of Fort Severn and the academic program has become more advanced to keep up with modern technology. In 1987, the Computing Sciences Accreditation Board (CSAB) granted accreditation for the Computer Science program.

The 21st Century promises many opportunities for growth. The Naval Academy will continue to provide state-of-the-art training and learning strategies and provide an environment that will properly train all of our officers to the expected standards and rigors of naval service. Newly commissioned officers will bring with them exceptional skills and abilities that blend and employ the diverse cultures, talents and experiences that each of our future leaders being to the Navy. The Naval Academy will continue to provide future leaders with the right foundation for success.

A spectacular **AERIAL VIEW OF THE ACADEMY** shows its unique location as it appears to be an integral part of Annapolis. You can clearly see the buildings of the Academy with the Maryland State House and the city of Annapolis in the background. The southern border to the left of the Academy is defined by Spa Creek and to the right is the Severn River, College Creek lies to the upper right.

TOUR OF THE YARD

Known as the Yard, the scenic Naval Academy comes to life in the photographs that follow. With its combination of early 20th-century and modern buildings, it is a blend of tradition and state-of-the-art technology that exemplifies today's Navy and Marine Corps. Historic monuments honoring naval heroes and events are located throughout the Yard. Old, green-patinated, bronze cannons can be seen around the Yard as well as benches, statues, plaques and other reminders of the rich history of the Navy, Marines and the Academy.

The majority of the 13 miles of roads are named after past superintendents. The officers' residences along Rodgers and Upshur Roads are known as "the parade field houses," as they border Worden Field, the parade field named after Rear Admiral John L. Worden, commander of the *USS Monitor* and a former superintendent. Porter Road, also known as "Captains' Row" is where the highest ranking officers and their families reside. There are more than 15 miles of walkways around the Yard, some of which are also named for past superintendents, such as Stribling Walk and Goldsborough Walk.

The Yard also is the final resting place of Revolutionary War naval hero John Paul Jones, whose words, "I have not yet begun to fight," have inspired generations of naval officers. His crypt is located beneath the Academy Chapel. The Zimmermann Bandstand was named after Bandmaster Charles A. Zimmermann who composed the Navy Song, "Anchors Aweigh" and led the Naval Academy Band for almost 30 years.

Elsewhere on the Yard, one can see numerous athletic facilities and fields which enable the midshipmen to participate in many different intercollegiate sports. A serene, tree-covered cemetery, dating back to 1869, four years after the Civil War, spills over the hill on the north shore where College Creek flows into the Severn. This is the resting place of officers of every rank, from fleet admiral to ensign, their wives and children.

The Academy has grown substantially in size since its inception in 1845. In 1847, the school doubled its original 10 acres through the attainment of neighboring property. Following the Civil War, Prospect Hill and Strawberry Hill farms, a total of 113 acres, were acquired across College Creek. By 1941, the Academy had grown to 245 acres. Dewey and Farragut Fields were created in 1960 by dredging the Severn River and Spa Creek. From its original 10 acres, it has grown to 338 acres.

Over the course of the last century, the appearance of the Academy changed immensely. An ambitious reconstruction plan began in 1899, designed by architect Ernest Flagg, when work on a new armory, Dahlgren Hall was begun. The building of MacDonough and Bancroft Halls followed soon afterwards. Flagg's plan included a new topography for the Yard, placing the chapel atop the highest point of land and facing the Severn River. Today, if you stand on the top step of the chapel and face the river, you can see the enormous Bancroft Hall to the right; to the left you can see some of the academic buildings surrounding Mahan Hall with its bell tower. Directly in front, you have a spectacular view of the river and a beautiful tree-shaded quadrangle of flower gardens.

The cornerstone of the Naval Academy Chapel was laid into place by Admiral Dewey in 1904. Flagg's extensive reconstruction continued through 1908. The Officers' Club was completed in 1905 and Bancroft Hall and Buchanan House were finished in 1906. In 1907, the Naval Academy Hospital and Administration Building opened, and Mahan, Sampson and Maury Halls were completed. Flagg's reconstruction showcases the largest group of Beaux Arts buildings in the United States. In 1913, a concrete bridge was erected across College Creek and during this same year, John Paul Jones' body was placed in its final resting place in a crypt beneath the chapel. Luce Hall was finished in 1920 and in 1929, work began on Hubbard Hall on the north bank of College Creek. Preble Hall, which houses the Naval Academy Museum, was opened in 1939, and in 1940, the chapel nave was extended to accommodate 2,500 worshipers.

The Yard again changed in the second half of the twentieth century. King Hall, the mess hall in Bancroft, received a new wing in 1952 and the seventh and eighth wings of Bancroft Hall were completed in 1959. Ricketts, Chauvenet and Michelson Halls were completed in the 1960's. In the 1970's, Nimitz Library, The Robert Crown Sailing Center, Rickover Hall and a student union in Dahlgren Hall were completed. Lejeune Hall is the physical education center which was constructed in 1982 and houses an Olympic-size swimming pool, wrestling loft and saunas. Alumni Hall was completed in 1991 and seats 6,000 in the round for basketball games, lectures and some concerts. The Bob Hope Performing Arts Center, which is created by lowering a stage and backdrop from the ceiling, seats 1,200.

The Academy is continually remodeled or has new facilities added to keep up with its needs and improve its academic, professional and sports programs. You will see new facilities such as the Wesley Brown Field House, new soccer stadium, new Jewish Chapel, the newly-renovated Museum and more.

BANCROFT HALL - Architect Ernest Flagg (1857-1947) designed Bancroft Hall in Beaux Arts style. One of the primary architectural characteristics which defines Flagg's buildings is the mansard roof, designed by French architect Nicolas Francois Mansart (1598-1666) as a way of using the upper story or attic of a building.

BANCROFT HALL is one of the world's largest dormitories and is home to more than 4000 midshipmen. It has 1,700 residential rooms, almost five miles of corridors and 33 acres of floor space. In addition to dorm rooms, there are offices, a barbershop, bank, travel office, restaurant, bookstore, uniform store, general store, laundromat, post office and full medical, dental, optometry and orthopedic clinics. It is open year-round and offers midshipmen all the basic facilities necessary for daily life.

BANCROFT HALL - Since 1906, Bancroft has been home to the Brigade of Midshipmen. Although the living areas of Bancroft are off-limits to visitors, several other areas are open to visitors, such as the vast Rotunda and Memorial Hall. From the Rotunda, visitors can see an example of a midshipman's room. Nearby stands the bust of a Native American named Tamanend which was a figurehead on the *USS Delaware.* Nicknamed "Tecumseh" by the midshipmen, this statue sports different colors during the year. Midshipmen paint him to commemorate various celebrations – football season, graduation, etc.

COLOR GUARD – Members of the Color Guard and the Brigade Commander and their staff are the only midshipmen who are allowed to pass through the center door of Bancroft Hall until after graduation. During each parade the Color Guard exits Bancroft Hall and joins the Brigade in "Tecumseh Court."

MEMORIAL HALL is one of the Academy's most hallowed places. This exquisite room contains exhibits, memorabilia and several rolls of honor, including lists of Academy alumni who were killed in action and of those awarded the Medal of Honor. The hall is adorned by two massive Czechoslovakian chandeliers in the main room, a smaller chandelier in the two side wings and a glorious skylight created from four hundred, eighty-nine panes of glass. The focal point of Memorial Hall is replica of the original battle flag bearing the words, "Don't Give up the Ship," used in 1813 by Commodore Oliver Hazard Perry to signal his forces in winning the Battle of Lake Erie. The original flag is located in the Naval Academy Museum.

BANCROFT HALL ROTUNDA – With its beautiful, marble-parquet floor, the Rotunda is the main entrance to Bancroft Hall and a central meeting place of the Academy. Large oil portraits of Secretary of the Navy George Bancroft, who founded the school in 1845, and President James K. Polk adorn its walls. A grand staircase from the Rotunda leads up to Memorial Hall.

THE CHAPEL IN THE 2009 BLIZZARD

U.S. NAVAL ACADEMY CHAPEL – The current chapel is the fourth revision of the Naval Academy Chapel. The first Chapel, located near the Tecumseh statue, was built in 1854 and sat 300 people. The second was used from 1868 to 1904, and both were demolished. The third chapel, designed by Ernest Flagg seated 1,200 and was built between 1904 and 1908. It was expanded in 1940, changing the basic design from a Greek cross to a Latin cross and doubling the seating capacity. It was refurbished in 2009 and given a cleaner appearance.

THE CHAPEL WITH SPRING FLOWERS

VIEW OF THE CHAPEL FROM EASTPORT

WEDDING AT THE NAVAL CHAPEL

THE CHAPEL RISES 200 FEET ABOVE THE YARD

U.S. NAVAL ACADEMY CHAPEL – No matter how one approaches Annapolis – by land, sea or air, its tiered dome dominates the skyline. Built on the highest ground at the Academy, the Naval Chapel is clearly visible just about everywhere. **NAVAL ACADEMY WEDDINGS** are a beautiful experience at the Naval Academy Chapel. More than 130 weddings take place in the main chapel every year.

LOOKING DOWN AT THE CHAPEL FROM THE DOME

MONTE MAXWELL AT THE CHAPEL ORGAN

TIFFANY WINDOW DEDICATED TO ADMIRAL DAVID DIXON PORTER

SOME OF THE PIPES OF THE MOELLER ORGAN

U.S. NAVAL ACADEMY CHAPEL - As one enters the sanctuary, the eye is drawn to the famous Porter window. Made by Louis C. Tiffany Studios, it is a memorial to Admiral David Dixon Porter. Presented in 1908, it shows Christ, his face illuminated by golden light, walking upon glistening waters. Monte Maxwell has been serving as the chapel organist since 1997. He is a graduate of Texas Christian University, the Curtis Institute and the Juilliard School.

THE LIGHTS IN THE DOME APPEAR ALMOST LIKE STARS

U.S. NAVAL ACADEMY CHAPEL – The dome rises above the altar and adds magical lighting to the Chapel. In addition to regular services, the Chapel hosts many weddings, baptisms, funerals and memorial services. The small lights in the dome appear to be stars when the lighting is right. The chapel organ, originally designed by Hutchings-Votey in 1908, was rebuilt and enhanced by the Moeller Organ Company in 1940 and later , the R. A. Colby Organ Company in 2012. The majestic gold facade pipes mask thousands of other organ pipes directly behind them.

ADMIRAL FARRAGUT WINDOWS

BUST OF JOHN PAUL JONES BY JEAN ANTOINE HOUDON

POW /MIA CANDLE IN ROW FIFTY-ONE

SIMILAR WINDOWS ARE DOWN BOTH SIDES OF THE CHAPEL

U.S. NAVAL ACADEMY CHAPEL – The Chapel is enhanced by the beauty of its many stained glass windows commemorating Biblical and Naval history. The candle in the Chapel is lit for the prisoners of war and those missing in action. Pew 51 is where the entrance to the chapel was before it was expanded in 1940. The bust of John Paul Jones is displayed in the crypt where his body entombed.

THE JOHN PAUL JONES COFFIN AND SURROUNDING COLUMNS OF ROYAL PYRENEES MARBLE

JOHN PAUL JONES CRYPT - The great naval leader of the American Revolution, Commodore John Paul Jones is entombed beneath the Chapel. Architect Whitney Warren (1864-1943) designed the space and sculptor Sylvain Salieres (1865-1920), who Warren brought to the U.S. from France to work on Grand Central Railroad Station in New York City, designed the sarcophagus, its seaweed decorations, the supporting bronze dolphins and the marble columns. The grand Antique des Pyrennes black and white marble was donated by France and cut in a shop in Baltimore for Salieres' design.

25

EXTERIOR OF THE COMMODORE URIAH P. LEVY CENTER

HOLOCUST TORAH

THE ARK IS FLANKED BY A WALL OF JERUSALEM STONE

THE LOBBY FEATURES A STAR OF DAVID WINDOW

THE COMMODORE URIAH P. LEVY CENTER AND JEWISH CHAPEL – Nestled in a courtyard formed by the seventh and eighth wings of Bancroft Hall, the Levy Center has become integral to Academy life. Dedicated for Jewish service and education in September of 2005, the Levy Center and Jewish Chapel had long been the dream of Jewish midshipmen. Central to the atrium's design is a twelve-foot Star of David. The atrium walls and a kiosk display the names of its many donors. A priceless collection of Torahs highlight the Chapel.

SERVICE IN JEWISH CHAPEL

THE COMMODORE URIAH P. LEVY CENTER AND JEWISH CHAPEL – The Chapel's four-story high ceiling, coated in silver leaf, gives the appearance that there is no ceiling at all. The curvature of the stone floor and placement of the furniture on the Chapel's first floor gives the impression that the center aisle is going uphill, symbolizing "Aliyah" (the Hebrew term for ascending the altar).

THE U.S. NAVAL ACADEMY MUSEUM – The Museum, founded in 1845, is among our nation's oldest museums. It collects, records, and uses in exhibitions historical and artistic objects promoting the proud heritage of the U.S. Navy and the Academy with an emphasis on the officer corps and those who have contributed their knowledge, skills and lives to the nation and mankind.

THE U.S. NAVAL ACADEMY MUSEUM – The museum contains more than fifty thousand historical items including ship models, manuscripts, paintings, weapons, prints, medals, uniforms and other treasures from famous naval ships, officers and historical incidents. The Museum also maintains records on all of the historical monuments and items found around the Yard.

MAHAN HALL - The bell tower of Mahan Hall has graced the Yard for over a century. Until 1973, Mahan Hall was home to the Naval Academy library. It is flanked on one side by Maury Hall and on the other by Sampson Hall. When its stage with its magnificent proscenium arch was completed in 1907, the midshipmen formally organized their theatrical company into what has been known ever since as the Masqueraders. They perform a drama or comedy in November and a musical in late February. The Hart Room is now a nicely furnished student-faculty lounge. It is one of the oldest buildings in the Yard.

MAHAN HALL - Completed in 1907, it was named after Rear Admiral Alfred Thayer Mahan, an extraordinary biographer and historian whose writings transformed naval strategy. His book, *The Influence of Sea Power Upon History*, was recognized internationally as a comprehensive dissertation on naval strategy. Mahan stressed the value of sea power in the world and ultimately influenced the policy-making of the United States and Germany leading up to the First World War.

BUCHANAN HOUSE - Completed in 1906, Buchanan House serves as the residence of the current Naval Academy superintendent. Buchanan House was named after Admiral Franklin Buchanan in 1976. Admiral Buchanan was appointed a midshipman in 1815 and became a commander in 1841. He was also the primary advisor to Secretary of the Navy George Bancroft in planning the Naval Academy and became the Academy's first superintendent.

BUCHANAN HOUSE - The Superintendent's residence sits next to the Naval Academy Chapel. It was designed by Architect Ernest Flagg in Beaux Arts style, who designed the architecture of Bancroft Hall, the chapel, Mahan, Maury and Sampson Halls, among others. Buchanan house has hosted some of the world's most distinguished individuals, such as heads of state, US presidents, foreign royalty and ambassadors, and has entertained more guests than any other official government residence except the White House. Special events are frequently held in the lovely gardens at the rear of the house.

MEXICAN MONUMENT

LEJEUNE MEMORIAL

MACEDONIAN MONUMENT

TRIPOLI MONUMENT

THE MEXICAN MONUMENT - a marble obelisk supported by a rectangular base and four upright cannons, is a memorial to four midshipmen who gave their lives during the Mexican War. **THE LEJEUNE MEMORIAL**-honors Lt. General John A. Lejeune, who was the 13th commandant of the Marine Corps. **THE MACEDONIAN MONUMENT** - is the figurehead of the British ship the HMS *Macedonian*, captured during the War of 1812. *Macedonian's* figurehead was a depiction of the bust of Alexander the Great. **THE TRIPOLI MONUMENT** - is among our nation's oldest military monuments and commemorates six naval officers who gave their lives in defending American commerce during the Barbary Wars.

TECUMSEH

THE GOAT

TECUMSEH

HERNDON MONUMENT

The most well-known monument in the yard is the figurehead from the bow of the *USS Delaware*. Nicknamed **"TECUMSEH,"** this bust of a Native American was originally carved in wood to represent Tamanend, a Delaware Chief. THE **HERNDON MONUMENT** is a 21 foot monument dedicated to Captain William Lewis Herndon, who is noted for rescuing 152 women and children while commanding a commercial mail steamer, then chose to stay with 400 other passengers as the ship went down during a hurricane. **THE GOAT** is a bronze goat that represents the Naval Academy's live mascot.

35

ZIMMERMAN BANDSTAND

VICE ADMIRAL LAWRENCE STATUE

MAST OF THE MAINE

THE SUBMARINE MEMORIAL

ZIMMERMAN BANDSTAND – This gazebo was named for Bandmaster Charles A. Zimmerman, the band director from 1887 – 1916. He composed a new piece of music for each graduating class. His most celebrated composition was for the Class of 1907, "Anchors Aweigh." **MAST OF THE "USS MAINE"** – The USS Maine sunk after a mysterious explosion while anchored in Havana Harbor at the beginning of the Spanish-American War. **THE SUBMARINE MEMORIAL** stands outside the second wing of Bancroft. It was unveiled and dedicated in October 2000, in honor of America's Submarine Centennial 1900-2000. **VICE ADMIRAL WILLIAM P. LAWRENCE STATUE** class of 1951, honors his service as the first naval aviator to fly twice the speed of sound, and he was a Superintendent of the Naval Academy.

ALUMNI HALL - Completed in 1991, Alumni Hall is named in honor of alumni who together contributed more than one-half of the construction cost. It can seat 6,500 in the round and boasts a 2,400 square-foot stage. Alumni Hall is the site of home games for Navy basketball, major lectures such as the Forrestal Lectures, and for a Distinguished Artist Series that has brought the New York Opera, Bolshoi Ballet, Annapolis Symphony Orchestra, and many great performances for the benefit of the Brigade and its guests.

DAHLGREN HALL - Once an armory, Dahlgren Hall is now an activity center and a place where midshipmen can entertain visitors. The Dry Dock Restaurant on premises is open to the public and seats 150. A working model of a B1 Wright Brother aeroplane flown in Annapolis is suspended from the ceiling at one end of the hall. The original was assembled here in the old armory and hauled out by midshipmen onto Farragut Field on September 7, 1911. Lieutenant John Rodgers, naval aviator number two, took off, flew over the academy for fifteen minutes, landed, refueled, and flew into Washington where he landed on the Mall.

OFFICER'S CLUB

ADMINISTRATION BUILDING

DAHLGREN HALL

LUCE HALL

THE ADMINISTRATION BUILDING houses the offices of the Superintendent and the Public Affairs Office. **DAHLGREN HALL** is comparable to a student union at civilian colleges. The Division of Professional Development, including seamanship and navigation, and a planetarium are located within **LUCE HALL**. **THE OFFICERS' CLUB** is a place where officers can entertain visitors and hold various functions.

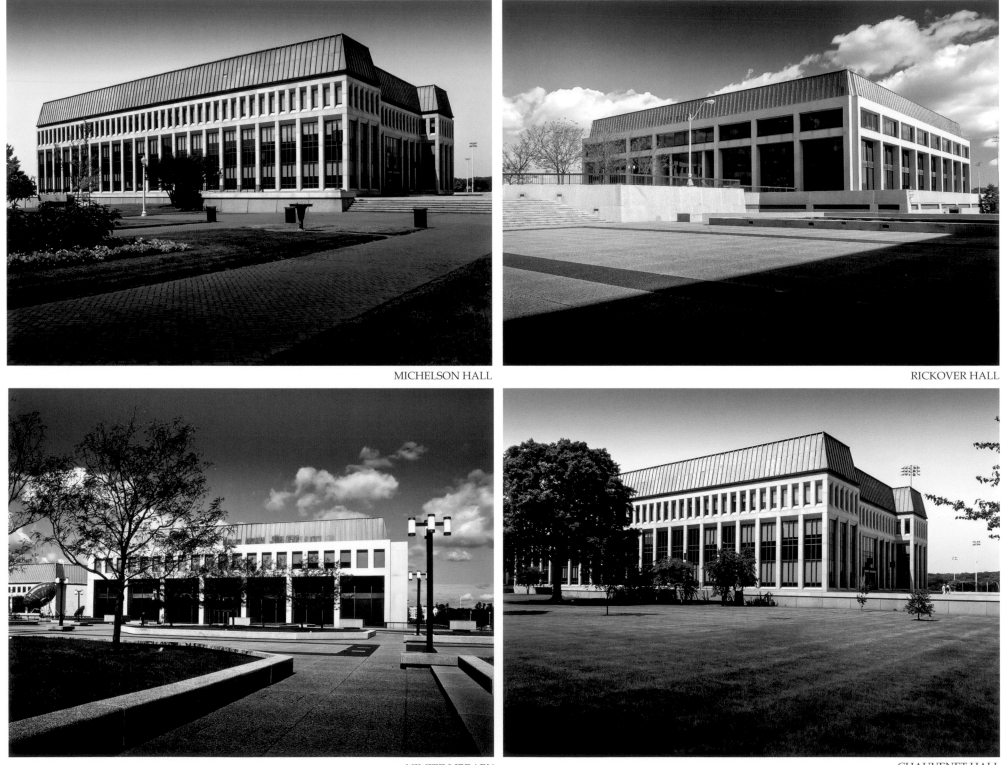

MICHELSON HALL

RICKOVER HALL

NIMITZ LIBRARY

CHAUVENET HALL

RICKOVER HALL houses the Division of Engineering and Weapons and contains the Academy's sophisticated laboratories. **THE NIMITZ LIBRARY** holds more than a half million books and can provide study-space for 1,500 midshipmen at one time. The Division of Mathematics and Science is housed in **CHAUVENET HALL** and its sister building **MICHELSON HALL** with more classrooms and laboratories.

MAURY HALL

SAMPSON HALL

WARD HALL

MAURY HALL

More classrooms and teachers' offices are located in **SAMPSON HALL.** Sampson Hall houses the Division of Humanities and Political Sciences which include the Departments of Economics, English, History, Language and Cultures and Political Science. **MAURY HALL** is the home to the Departments of Electrical and Computer Engineering and Systems Engineering. It also features a spiral staircase with a missile at the bottom. **WARD HALL** is dedicated to computer sciences classrooms and laboratories.

GLENN WARNER SOCCER FACILITY

HALSEY FIELD HOUSE

LEJEUNE HALL

MAX BISHOP STADIUM, TERWILLINGER BROTHERS FIELD

THE GLENN WARNER SOCCER FACILITY is one of the finest college soccer facilities in the nation. **HALSEY FIELD HOUSE** has more than two acres of indoor surface area with facilities for basketball, track, tennis, squash and weight-lifting. **LEJEUNE HALL** is a physical education center complete with an Olympic-size indoor pool and diving complex, as well as saunas, and a wrestling loft and conditioning area. **TERWILLIGER BROTHERS FIELD** at **MAX BISHOP STADIUM** is the third NCAA baseball facility to have FieldTurf on the entire field, excluding the pitcher's mound and home plate. It has a chair-back seating capacity of 1,500.

WESLEY A. BROWN FIELD HOUSE is a 140,000-square-foot multi-function athletic facility that serves as the home for the men's and women's track & field programs, the primary location for Navy volleyball matches and an indoor practice facility for the football and lacrosse teams. It is a unique combination of a 76,000-square-foot retractable Magic Carpet Astroturf system and a Mondo track surface with hydraulically controlled banked curves. It is dedicated to Commander Wesley A. Brown, the first African-American to graduate from the Naval Academy in 1949.

43

ALUMNI HOUSE/OGLE HALL - The two-story brick house is two blocks from Gate 3 of the Naval Academy. It was built in 1739 by Dr. William Stevenson. In 1747, the house was rented to Governor Samuel Ogle, and it served as the official Governor's Mansion. It is now the home of the Naval Academy Alumni Association and Foundation.

ALUMNI HOUSE/OGLE HALL - After serving as Governor's Mansion, the house was deeded to Ogle's son, Benjamin, who made some additions. After the Civil War, when Vice Admiral David Dixon Porter became superintendent of the Naval Academy, his son, Theodoric Porter raised his family at Ogle Hall, and the house stayed in the Porter family for more than forty years. In 1944, one of the Porter daughters sold Ogle Hall to the Naval Academy Alumni Association. In a dedication ceremony in 1945, Ogle Hall became officially known as Alumni House.

CAPTAIN'S ROW

VISITOR'S CENTER GIFT SHOP

ZIMMERMAN BAND STAND

GUIDED TOURS OF CAMPUS

CAPTAINS' ROW is home to the Academy's highest ranking officers and their families. **THE VISITORS' CENTER GIFT SHOP** provides visitors with an official United States Naval Academy shopping experience. All proceeds from the sale of tours and merchandise benefit the Brigade of Midshipmen activities. **ZIMMERMAN BANDSTAND** is named for Bandmaster Charles A. Zimmerman, the band director from 1887 – 1916. Visitors tour the Naval Academy with guided tours starting at the Visitors' Center.

THE ARMEL-LEFTWICH VISITOR CENTER - The Visitor Center is the first stop on a visit to the Naval Academy. Information specialists welcome visitors to view the 13-minute film, The Call to Serve, and to take a guided walking tour with a professional, certified guide.

THE BRIGADE OF MIDSHIPMEN - have developed and executed a document known as the Honor Treatise of the Brigade of Midshipmen. The Treatise is a statement directly from the Brigade conveying what they strive to achieve and who they are. It is a statement of their vision of themselves and the Fleet. This document underscores the commitment of the Brigade to living a life of honor and their dedication to doing that which is right.

MIDSHIPMEN'S LIFE

Induction or "I" Day is indelibly etched in the memory of every man or woman who has attended the United States Naval Academy. Every summer approximately 1100 men and women from all over the country arrive in Annapolis to be inducted into the Naval Academy. Crossing the threshold from civilians to "midshipmen in training," each faces a new world where the limits of individual capabilities are stretched and where the importance of trusting, respecting and depending on fellow classmates is imperative.

The instant they arrive, the "plebes" begin moving in a constant flow from station to station. Each new midshipman picks up a name-tag, receives a vision check, and has blood drawn, shots administered and additional medical and dental exams performed. It is that first visit to the barber's chair when all male plebes are shaved and all female plebes receive "chin-length" cuts and then don their uniforms that transforms this group of individuals into midshipmen.

The transformation from civilian teenager to midshipman, to Navy or Marine officer occurs differently for each man or woman who makes it through their training at the Naval Academy. Through the careful planning, teaching, training, enforcement of regulations and the high integrity of every Academy officer and staff member, the midshipmen have the opportunity to experience exceptional academic and military training that prepares them for command leadership in a field of their choice.

The first year, Plebe Year, is the most difficult for many and sets the tempo for all four years. The philosophy "he who would lead must first learn to follow" is the key to the plebe's life. Purposefully overloaded, plebes quickly learn to follow orders, prioritize wisely and use every second of their time appropriately and productively.

As "youngsters" in their second year, the metamorphosis continues with fewer regulations and more responsibility until as "firsties" in their fourth year, they have the most freedom, and the most responsibility. Some "firsties" are selected as Brigade leaders, who are responsible for supervising all plebe activities and enforcing the Honor Code.

Commanded and instructed by upperclassmen, all new plebes learn how to properly salute military officers, how to properly wear their hats, and how to stand at attention and at ease. It is made abundantly clear that there is no room for anyone at the Academy who would lie, cheat, steal or tolerate those who do. The moral shades of grey that exist on the outside are not acceptable within the walls of the Yard. This Honor Code of behavior is taken more seriously than any midshipman's own self-interest. Ultimately, the new plebes march to their new home, Bancroft Hall, among the largest college dormitories in the world, housing all of the more than 4,000 midshipmen.

Plebes go through the most rigorous training during their first six weeks at the Academy. Midshipmen have a lot to learn. As if demanding calisthenics are not enough, they must memorize necessary information; take and follow orders; keep their rooms and uniforms in order; and know where they are supposed to be during every minute of the day.

Days start early, with reveille at five-thirty a.m. After early morning calisthenics and runs around the Yard, the young midshipmen return to Bancroft Hall, and within ten to fifteen minutes, have taken a shower, put on a fresh uniform, learned the menus for the morning, noon and evening meals, shined their shoes, wiped off their covers, read three newspaper articles and have hurried on their way to morning formation.

All plebes learn a new way of walking and talking. They are taught how to "chop," placing the left foot forward, then the right, very quickly. "Go Navy, Sir!" is heard echoing through the halls along with the pounding of short, double-time steps (one hundred and sixty to one hundred and eighty steps per minute). They have a determined and fixed gaze as they square corners and learn the Navy way to walk.

Later, while in formation outside King Hall, "chow calls" begins. Each plebe must rapidly and accurately recite where the formation is (inside or outside), the uniform for the formation, the menu for the meal, the midshipman and officer on duty for the day, the week's professional topic and the day's major events in the yard! A seemingly endless day ends with taps around ten p.m.

Those who have what it takes persist through the rigorous physical and mental training day after day. They persist and begin to recognize the significance of the decision to serve their country as Navy or Marine officers. It is a life-altering and noble path of service mirroring the more than 67,000 others who have gone before them.

What is the purpose of all of this hardship? Naval and Marine officers must have the fortitude and ability to function well under physical, emotional and mental stress. Of all of the valuable lessons taught at the Academy during the four year apprenticeship, this is the one that could mean the difference between life and death. An officer who waivers or folds-up under stress, be it in battle, on or under water, on land or in the air, is not only endangering his own life, but the lives of those under his command, and possibly the lives of the citizens of America.

While it takes a particular type of person to get through four years at the Academy, all midshipmen are not alike. They mirror the diversity that makes our nation great. But there is a common thread, one that does not show up in statistics. Besides having been outstanding students and leaders in their high schools and communities, midshipmen are patriots who are driven to excel and thrive when challenged to grow intellectually, physically and morally.

The responsibility for the entire Brigade's professional training and day-to-day activities is overseen by a midshipmen command structure, headed by a first-class midshipmen designated Brigade Commander. The Brigade Commander is carefully chosen for outstanding performance as a leader. The Commandant of Midshipmen, an active duty Navy or Marine Corps officer of Captain or Colonel rank (often promoted to Rear Admiral or Brigadier General while in the position), is responsible for the day-to-day life of the midshipmen.

In addition to academics, midshipmen have access to more than seventy Extracurricular Activities that give them the opportunity to participate in brigade support, musical/theatrical, heritage, community service, religious, professional and athletic activities.

Their lives are highly structured, beginning with reveille and ending with lights out. They wear uniforms for just about everything they do, must keep their uniforms in regulation condition, march to meals, stand watches and be prepared for military inspection of their quarters at any time. They are to be applauded for choosing the path less traveled; a path that will offer challenges beyond their expectations and the greater rewards that come from knowing they are prepared to lead with honor and integrity as Naval Academy graduates.

CHAPLAIN WELCOMING NEW PLEBES

WHAT'S YOUR NAME?

NEW HAT NEW CLOTHES

PLEBE GETTING HAIRCUT

I-Day - In a period of less than twenty-four hours, plebes shed all traces of civilian life. On Induction Day, they get a military haircut; pick up their first issue of uniforms and hats; and begin learning how to stand, salute and take orders. All the new plebes are welcomed to the Naval Academy by one of the Chaplains.

PLEBE SUMMER BEGINS ON I-DAY – Plebes begin basic training. They learn to take and follow orders, and are quickly transformed from a group of individuals who do not know each other into a company of midshipmen who wear the same uniform, operate as a group and begin to depend on each other.

NEW FIRSTIES READY TO TRAIN NEW PLEBES – Supervised by Navy and Marine Corps officers and enlisted men and women, midshipmen in the first class are ready to train the new plebes on all facets of becoming midshipmen.

PLEBES GETTING NEW UNIFORMS

PLEBES LEARNING TO SALUTE

PLEBES READING *REEF POINTS*

CEREMONIAL OATH OF OFFICE

The small book they hold is called **REEF POINTS**, a manual for plebes that functions as a Plebe Summer Bible. It contains helpful tidbits of information to ease the transition to military life. Plebes learn quickly how to walk, talk, stand, salute and recite information from *Reef Points*. The formal Oath of Office is Administered at the end of I-day. Plebes also sign a legal Oath of Office earlier in the day.

PLEBE SUMMER - is different from anything these young men and women have ever experienced. It begins in July and lasts a grueling six weeks. During the nearly seventeen-hour days, plebes endure heat and humidity as they begin with early morning exercises. The mental and physical pressure placed on their shoulders requires them to learn to think and act correctly, swiftly and intuitively.

PLEBE SUMMER - The day begins at 5:30 am with calisthenics and a run. During Plebe Summer, each plebe is issued an M-14 rifle for which they are responsible and carry with them during exercise and marching. They learn to shoot rifles, march in formation and get a variety of military training.

WORKING BLUE

SUMMER WHITE

THE UNIFORM becomes who you are and is impeccably kept and worn with pride. To the novice, uniforms may all appear similar, but to anyone in the Navy or the Naval Academy, a uniform speaks volumes. It states your rank, your position and awards won. Insignia are awarded to midshipmen for various accomplishments.

SERVICE KHAKI

SERVICE DRESS BLUE

Class and rank insignia allow one to identify a midshipman's status quickly. Midshipmen first-class wear one stripe around each sleeve, parallel to the cuff. Second-class wear two stripes on the left sleeve, diagonal. Third-class wear one diagonal stripe on the left sleeve and fourth class wear no stripe at all. Midshipmen first-class officers wear a five-point star on both sleeves above the stripe(s). A Midshipman Captain wears six stripes on the sleeve of the Blue Service and Full Dress Blue Jacket, a Midshipmen Commander wears five, a Midshipmen Lieutenant Commander wears four stripes, a Midshipmen Lieutenant wears three stripes, a Midshipmen Lieutenant Junior Grade wears two stripes and a Midshipman Ensign wears one stripe.

57

SERVICE DRESS WHITE

NAVY WORKING UNIFORM

Shirt collar insignia also indicate class with midshipmen first-class wearing an eagle insignia on both collars, second-class wear an anchor insignia on both, third-class wear an anchor on the right collar only and midshipmen fourth-class wear no insignia. Star insignia are awarded to midshipmen for various accomplishments. Those who have made the Superintendent's List wear a gold star, a silver star is awarded to those midshipmen achieving athletic excellence and a bronze star is awarded to those who have made the Dean's List. There are many additional ribbons and medals which may be worn by those who have earned them.

FEMALE: DINNER DRESS WHITE JACKET, MALE: DINNER DRESS BLUE JACKET

FEMALE: INFANTRY DRESS GOLF, MALE: INFANTRY DRESS FOXTROT

White Works are worn for Plebe Summer Meal Formations, Camouflage Utilities are worn as directed for specific training. Marine Corps Capstone Course Instructors have the option of requiring first-class to wear utilities to class. If so, they are worn to class only, and are not worn to formations or inspections. Working Khakis are worn when prescribed for Summer Cruise, Plebe Summer Detailers, Summer Training Programs and Summer School Classes. Of course, athletic wear is worn when participating in athletic activities.

BANCROFT HALL LIVING QUARTERS - A rite of passage for plebes is "squaring corners" and "sounding off." All turns in Bancroft hallways are made at ninety degrees while saying "Go Navy, sir! Beat Army, sir!" Deck plates are metal squares on the floors of Bancroft corridors at major "chopping" intersections where plebes turn or square their corners. Upperclassmen may stop plebes at almost any time of the day during Plebe Year and order them to immediately recite designated military information a plebe is required to know.

FEMALE MIDSHIPMEN ROOM

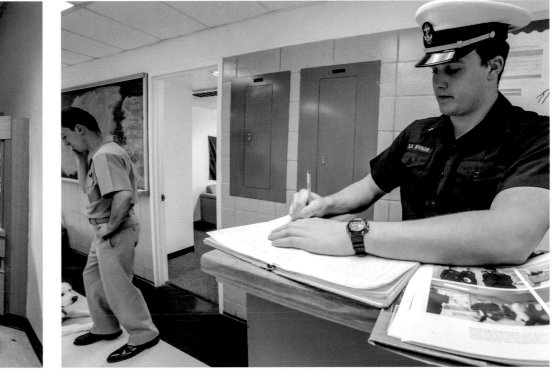

COMPANY MATE OF THE DECK SCHEDULING THE COMPANY

SENIOR ENLISTED ADVISOR AND COMPANY OFFICER

INSPECTION AND ROLL CALL INSIDE OF BANCROFT

BANCROFT HALL - This is a view of Bancroft that outsiders don't see. Midshipmen can share a room with two, three and sometimes, four others. Their rooms are kept flawless, as they are expected to be ready for inspection at any time of the day or night. They learn to wax the deck, wash the showers, windows and bulkheads and put away their clothes in a particular fashion. During inspections, upperclassmen examine every inch of the room with a white glove and a black sock. A Navy or Marine Corps officer and a senior enlisted man or women supervise each company.

61

VICE ADMIRAL TED CARTER, SUPERINTENDENT, AT THE HERNDON MONUMENT

NAVAL ACADEMY SUPERINTENDENT AND THE COMMANDANT OF MIDSHIPMEN

CHAIN OF COMMAND At the top of the Chain of Command at the Naval Academy is the Superintendent. Next in line is the Commandant of Midshipmen followed by the Deputy Commandant, the Company Officer and a senior enlisted leader. The midshipmen follow the orders of all of the above. **KING HALL** is a 65,000 square-foot dining room. The Brigade of more than four thousand midshipmen dine in the huge wardroom at one time, three times a day, where freshly prepared meals are served. Of the one hour allotted for each meal, midshipmen are required to be in King Hall for twenty minutes and then they can dismiss themselves. Usually they eat quickly so that they have forty minutes to study before their next class.

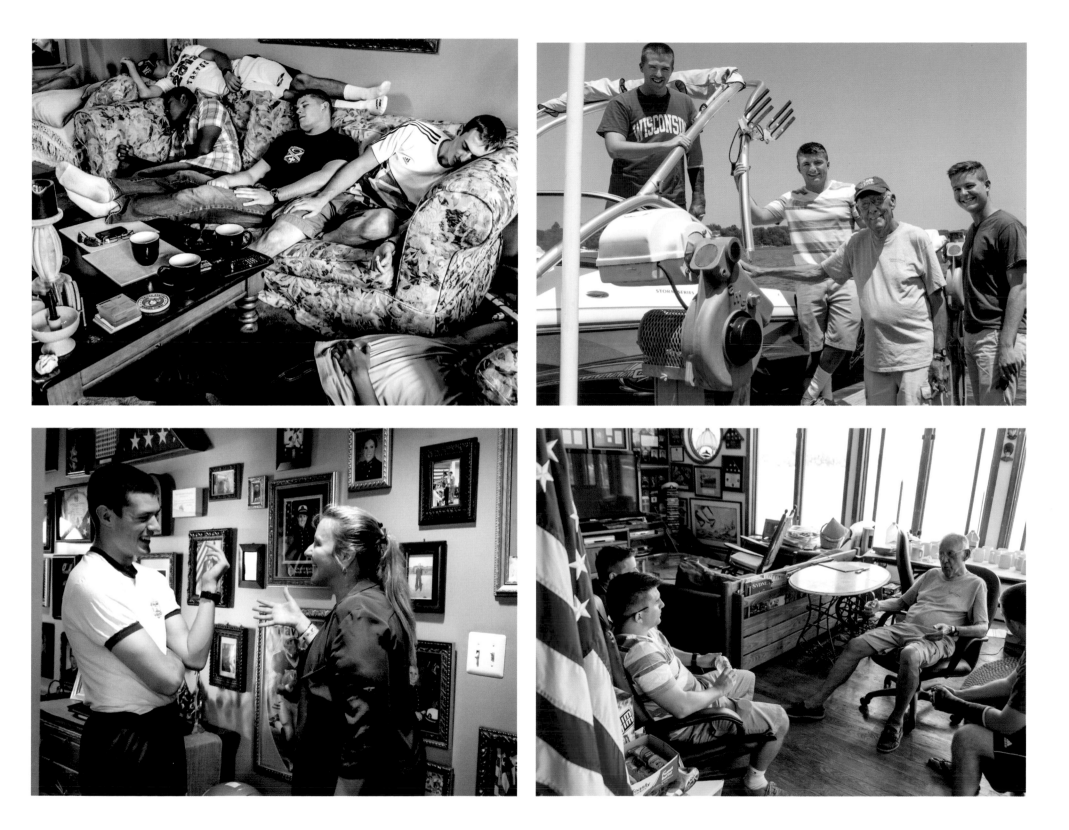

MIDSHIPMEN SPONSOR PROGRAM - There are 2,100 residences in the Annapolis area that open their homes to midshipmen. 95 percent of the brigade of midshipmen participate in the program. Every midshipman has a designated sponsor he or she may visit when on liberty. Sponsors are especially appreciated during plebe year and routinely become long-term friends and confidants. These sponsors are volunteers and receive no compensation.

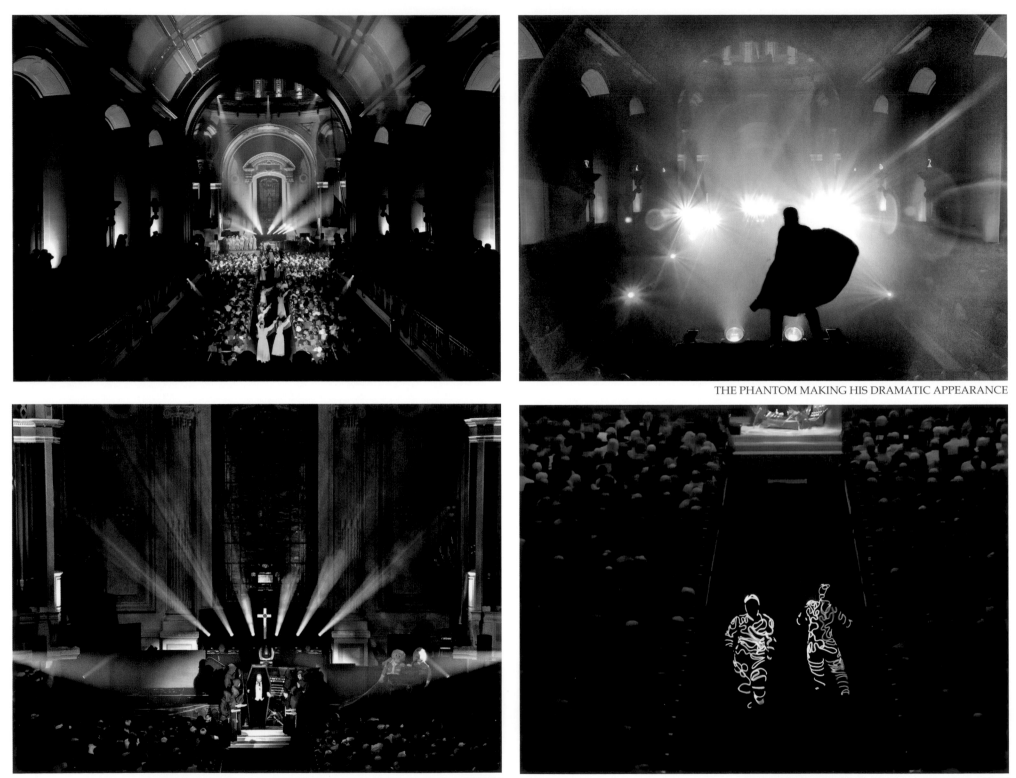

THE PHANTOM MAKING HIS DRAMATIC APPEARANCE

MONTE MAXWELL MAKES HIS DRAMATIC ENTRANCE IN A COFFIN

ELECTRIFIED MIDSHIPMEN DANCE IN THE AISLES

HALLOWEEN/ALL SAINT'S DAY AT THE NAVAL ACADEMY is celebrated in the Naval Academy Chapel with a special show with a Mardi Gras flair, complete with costumes and fanfare. A spoof of the "Phantom of the Opera" is presented with the Phantom appearing in different location of the chapel. The concert features Monte Maxwell, organist and Director of Chapel Music, rising out of a coffin at the beginning of the concert.

THE PHANTOM READY FOR HIS ENTRANCE

HALLOWEEN/ALL SAINT'S DAY AT THE NAVAL ACADEMY - The normally somber chapel comes alive with electrifying music with the multi-faceted talents of the midshipmen dancing and singing. The dramatic show is designed and produced by Monte Maxwell, Naval Academy Chapel Organist. The concert draws some 4,000 concert-goers annually. The show is a must-see for many people in Annapolis.

NAVAL ACADEMY VS. ST. JOHN'S CROQUET MATCH

FORMAL DANCES IN ALUMNI HALL

NAVAL ACADEMY VS. ST. JOHN'S CROQUET MATCH

MAG - MIDSHIPMEN ACTION GROUP-CLOTHING DRIVE

NAVAL ACADEMY VS. ST. JOHN'S COLLEGE - The annual croquet game between the Naval Academy and St. Johns College has become a tradition and is taken very seriously. The midshipmen wear casual clothes and the "Johnnies" wear mock Naval Uniforms. **FORMAL DANCES** are held in Alumni Hall with midshipmen in their dinner dress uniforms and civilian dates wear proper formal attire. **MIDSHIPMEN ACTION GROUP (MAG)** midshipmen support worthy causes and projects in the surrounding communities. In the above photograph MAG is supporting the Franciscan Center with a clothing drive.

RETIRING THE FLAG

PLEBE PARENTS WEEKEND

THE SILENT DRILL TEAM

PLEBE PARENTS WEEKEND

DAILY DUTIES – Midshipmen are assigned to do most of the day-to day activities at the Naval Academy. Before sundown, these midshipmen lower the flag, fold it and retire it for the day. **THE SILENT DRILL TEAM " THE COMMANDANT'S OWN"** Midshipmen can participate in many clubs that allow them to develop new skills. **PLEBE PARENTS' WEEKEND** is much like Parents' Weekend at any college. This is the first time parents are able to visit their sons or daughters since waving good-bye during Plebe Summer.

Outside of each classroom in Chauvenet, Michelson, Rickover, Maury and Sampson Halls, there is a place for midshipmen to leave their hats and book-bags.

ACADEMICS

The United States Naval Academy is much more than a display of impeccably uniformed future Naval and Marine officers parading around the grounds and shouting, "Go Navy! Beat Army!" The Naval Academy is nationally recognized as a four-year college that offers excellent academic and professional training. The curriculum is demanding, and the Naval Academy offers ample opportunity for each individual to explore his or her own academic aptitudes and interests.

The academic program begins with a core curriculum that includes courses in engineering, science, mathematics and the humanities. The Division of Engineering and Weapons includes: Aerospace Engineering; Computer Engineering; Electrical Engineering; General Engineering; Mechanical Engineering; Naval Architecture; Ocean Engineering and Systems Engineering. The Division of Mathematics and Science includes: Chemistry; Computer Science; General Science; Information Technology; Mathematics; Oceanography; Physics; Quantitative Economics and Operations Research. The Division of Humanities and Social Sciences includes: Arabic; Chinese; Economics; English; History and Political Science. Minors in French, German, Spanish, Russian and Japanese are also offered. Selection of a major occurs at the end of the plebe year. For four years, midshipmen will persist through 140 credits of academics required for graduation compared to 120 for most civilian colleges. In addition, they endure more than 2,000 hours of military and professional training, not to mention strenuous daily physical training.

The Naval Academy provides an excellent learning environment with a student to faculty ratio of 8:1. The faculty is comprised of an equal mix of civilian and military professors. All civilian professors hold a doctorate degree while military faculty members hold at least a master's.

There are numerous national scholastic honor societies at the Naval Academy and midshipmen who excel academically may earn membership in these societies. The Trident Scholar Program provides an opportunity for midshipmen to engage in independent study and research. During their third year, outstanding students are selected to participate in the program, and in their fourth year, the first-class scholars conduct independent research in their area of interest. They work closely with an expert in the field who acts as their faculty advisor. Trident Scholars carry a reduced formal course load to give them the time necessary to conduct in-depth research and prepare a thesis.

Midshipmen who are in the top ten percent of their class graduate with distinction. Honors students who complete a thesis or research project and orally defend it before a panel of faculty members graduate with honors. Midshipmen who have completed Academy course requirements early through validation or overloading can begin work toward a masters' degree at nearby universities, including University of Maryland, Johns Hopkins University, and Georgetown University. Each year, about twenty midshipmen start graduate work during first-class year and complete their master's degree within seven months after graduating. The field of study is selected from Navy-approved graduate education programs.

The Naval Academy's philosophy of education stresses individual attention to students with highly qualified faculty members who are strongly committed to teaching. The same professor who lectures in the classroom and supervises experiments in the lab also provides extra instruction sessions after the normal class periods.

Midshipmen are encouraged to be active in some of the many extracurricular activities offered at the Academy that span a variety of interests. Midshipmen have an opportunity to join academic and professional organizations as well as organizations that center around heritage. Midshipmen also have the opportunity to compete in Varsity, Club or Recreational Sports. Spirit activities such as cheerleading, Color Guard and Silent drill are also available for interested individuals.

Ethical and moral development is essential to a midshipman's education. No matter what midshipmen do later in life, the U.S. Naval Academy sharpens their talents and provides experiences that prepare them for success as future leaders.

MATHEMATICS AND SCIENCE – CHEMISTRY These photos take you into the chemistry laboratories where midshipmen work with professors and other midshipmen to complete various experiments. All Chemistry majors take required courses in organic, inorganic, analytical and physical chemistry and biochemistry. Ten slots are offered to midshipmen for pre-medical programs and they are able to attend medical school through the Navy.

MATHEMATICS AND SCIENCE - CHEMISTRY - Chemistry is an experimental science, and many hours are devoted to laboratory work. All of the facilities at the Naval Academy are state-of-the-art and provide an atmosphere where experiments can be conducted with precision and accuracy.

MATHEMATICS AND SCIENCE - COMPUTER SCIENCE - The Academy is one of our nation's most advanced computer science/information-technology campuses. The computer science courses give midshipmen a strong foundation in the main areas of computer science with a focus on naval applications. There are laboratories with high-end personal computers used for instructional support and are networked for local and remote access.

MATHEMATICS AND SCIENCE - MATHEMATICS - The mathematics major teaches logical and critical thinking, and problem-solving. These abilities are invaluable to Navy and Marine Corps officers. Nearly half the faculty of the Naval Academy is made up of civilians. Civilian professors must hold a doctorate degree.

MATHEMATICS AND SCIENCE -OCEANOGRAPHY - Midshipmen receive hands-on instruction in oceanography both in the classroom and on the water. Oceanography involves the study of meteorology, geophysics, physics, chemistry, biology and geology as they relate to the ocean environment.

MATHEMATICS AND SCIENCE - PHYSICS - A midshipman is working one-on-one with the professor on a particle accelerator in a physics laboratory. The study of physics lays a foundation for work in a broad range of fields. The integrated reasoning of physics is essential in problem-solving.

THE TEMPEST WILLIAM SHAKESPEARE

HUMANITIES AND SOCIAL SCIENCES - ENGLISH - The English department provides opportunities for midshipmen to use their talents and creativity as well as explore the roots of the language. Here, the "Masqueraders" take a bow.

THE IMPORTANCE OF BEING EARNEST OSCAR WILDE

TITUS ANDRONICUS WILLIAM SHAKESPEARE

HUMANITIES AND SOCIAL SCIENCES - ENGLISH - English in the classroom and on stage. Midshipmen explore techniques in oral and written communication. The effectiveness of an officer includes creativity, communication skills and independent thinking which are strongly encouraged in the English classrooms.

HUMANITIES AND SOCIAL SCIENCES - HISTORY - Midshipmen learn in many ways – lecture, webcasts, current media and presentations from active military personnel. The study of history provides the opportunity to examine our past and to evaluate and understand mankind through the ages. In addition, students learn to draw conclusions and express them clearly and concisely.

HUMANITIES AND SOCIAL SCIENCES - ECONOMICS - The Economics major acquaints midshipmen with micro- and macro- economic theory, quantitative methods in economics, economic problem-solving and international economic relations. Students also learn how various changes affect the market and financial systems.

HUMANITIES AND SOCIAL SCIENCES - LANGUAGES - Midshipmen have opportunities to learn Arabic, Chinese, German, French, Spanish, Russian and Japanese. Midshipmen not only develop communication skills in these languages, they also learn aspects of the cultures to help them understand the people and societies of these countries.

HUMANITIES AND SOCIAL SCIENCES - POLITICAL SCIENCE - The study of political science helps students understand the structure and functions of domestic and international political systems, emphasizing familiarity with the Constitution each midshipman has sworn to defend. The FBI agent who interrogated Sadam Hussein while he was in prison explains how important it is to form a bond with the prisoner in order to extract information from him or her.

ENGINEERING AND WEAPONS - WEAPONS AND SYSTEMS ENGINEERING - The Naval Academy has been rated number one for more than ten years for its systems engineering program. It encompasses electronics, mechanics, automatic control, computers and simulation to provide an overall understanding of the analysis and design of complete engineering systems. In addition, midshipmen learn about all types of weapons in the classroom, laboratories and rifle range.

ENGINEERING AND WEAPONS - ELECTRIC ENGINEERING AND COMPUTER ENGINEERING -
This department offers a solid grounding in the fundamentals of electrical engineering and an opportunity to investigate concepts in advanced communications systems, digital computer systems, fiber optic systems, microwaves and instrumentation.

ENGINEERING AND WEAPONS - MECHANICAL ENGINEERING - This is one of the most diversified programs, offering education in mechanical engineering that prepares its graduates to assume responsibilities in any of the warfare specialties in the Navy or Marine Corps. Graduates will be responsible for the operation and maintenance of high technology weapons systems. The first course ever in mechanical engineering was established at the Naval Academy in 1874.

CYBER SECURITY - As technology advances, cyber security has become more challenging and is now a major at the Naval Academy. A new building is under construction to make room for the necessary equipment, classrooms and laboratories needed to continue the expansion this area of concentration.

ENGINEERING - NAVAL ARCHITECTURE AND OCEAN ENGINEERING - A special combination of knowledge, experience, art and engineering is needed to design and build a ship. Naval architecture students learn how to convert functional requirements into a suitable cost-effective design. This 380-foot Tow Tank is used to test models of various ships, submarines, hydrofoils, sailboats, etc. It is also used to study wave motions and forces, without the use of models.

ENGINEERING - NAVAL ARCHITECTURE AND OCEAN ENGINEERING - Students of ocean engineering learn how to use the ocean environment most effectively to plan design and build coastal and offshore structures and underwater vehicles. The Tow Tank, equipped with two towing carriages, a dual flap wave-maker, a mechanism for maneuvering experiments, fans for simulating over-water winds. It is used to perform various seakeeping tests such as open water propeller tests, 3-D wake surveys and various tests of fixed and floating ocean structures using basic ocean wave mechanics.

ENGINEERING - AEROSPACE ENGINEERING - The aerospace engineering curriculum is structured to produce officers who will serve in the forefront of the inception, development and employment of Navy and space assets. The Naval Academy has its own satellite to study satellite attitude dynamics. Midshipmen can monitor it from their own laboratory. Wind tunnel experiments help midshipmen determine how a craft will react under certain conditions.

ENGINEERING - AEROSPACE ENGINEERING - Aerospace engineering students study aerospace engineering topics including aerodynamics, propulsion, aerospace structures, flight structures and flight mechanics. In the wind tunnel, midshipmen experiment with a prop to determine the proper positioning for airplane lift. There are 53 astronauts that have graduated from the Naval Academy, this is more than any other school in the world.

SURFACE SHIPS - Learning how to move a craft from one point to another and calculate your location are critical skills learned in professional development. The Professional Development Division readies midshipmen for service in the Navy and Marine Corps. The Professional Development Programs offer midshipmen hands-on experience in the field. The photo above is of the *USS Mitscher* (DDG-57), an Arliegh Burke Class guided missile destroyer arriving in Naval Station Mayport, Florida.

PROFESSIONAL TRAINING

The Professional Development Division develops midshipmen both academically and professionally on all things pertinent to military life. It consists of two teaching departments: Leadership, Ethics and Law (military) and Seamanship and Navigation. Each of these departments offers core-curriculum and elective courses. The non-academic departments that give midshipmen the opportunity to learn outside of the classroom are the Department of Professional Programs and the Department of Sailing Programs.

There are a number of courses offered in Seamanship and Navigation. For example, the Fundamentals of Naval Science teaches midshipmen fourth-class about the basics of seamanship, "rules of the road", navigation, damage control and maneuvering, and includes several opportunities for first-hand learning aboard Yard Patrol Craft. In the Navigation & Piloting course, midshipmen third-class get further instruction in basic piloting and an introduction to electronic, celestial and terrestrial navigation. Strategy and Tactics teaches midshipmen second-class about the development of maritime strategy and offers midshipmen the opportunity to apply these basic tactics in computer generated scenarios. In the service-specific Capstone course, soon-to-graduate midshipmen first-class learn what to expect from their chosen career paths. The introduction to life as a surface warfare officer, submariner, aviator, Marine or SEAL is a fitting culmination of four years of professional training.

The Department of Leadership, Ethics and Law presents a core of required courses, as well as electives in leadership, law, psychology, ethics and philosophy. All have the common objective of preparing midshipmen to lead as officers by providing the necessary principles and practical information to develop effective personal leadership styles. Leadership courses are the cornerstone of the department, focusing on developing leadership practices consistent with the highest standards of professional ethics to enhance mission accomplishment and provide for high unit morale. The core courses also arm future junior officers with the practical legal information they will need in the fleet regarding discipline and military justice, law of the sea and the law of armed conflict. Psychology elective courses are designed to help midshipmen learn and understand what motivates others and themselves.

As a part of their professional development, all midshipmen participate in four years of honor education. The Honor Concept requires the highest standards of personal integrity and focuses on doing what is right as opposed to simply not breaking the rules. Lying, cheating and stealing are not tolerated and may be cause for "separation" from the Naval Academy. The Honor System is completely overseen by midshipmen. Decisions about punishment are made by the Commandant of Midshipmen and the Superintendent. In 1994 a group of midshipmen developed an Honor Treatise that further demonstrates the commitment of the Brigade and the Naval Academy to moral and ethical conduct. Part of The Honor Treatise states, "It is our responsibility to develop a selfless sense of duty that demands excellence both of ourselves and those with whom we serve. We must honor our loyalties without compromising our ultimate obligation to the truth . . .. We believe that those with the strongest moral foundation will be the leaders who best reflect the legacy of the Naval Academy. This is our call as midshipmen; it is a mission we proudly accept."

On Induction Day (I-Day), plebes take the Oath of Office, but may not fully understand the importance or weightiness of it. During Plebe Summer, plebes take fifteen honor education and character development lessons, after which they have a better understanding of the intent and purpose of the Oath of Office. During Parents' Weekend, plebes participate in a rite of passage which marks the transition from learning about honor to living it. During an Honor Affirmation Ceremony, plebes reaffirm the Oath and formally declare their goal to live according to the Honor Concept and the Honor Treatise of the Brigade.

The Department of Professional Programs oversees three areas: the summer training programs, management of technical programs and the assignment of graduating midshipmen to the Navy and Marine Corps. The management of technical programs includes the maintenance and operation of fleet warfare simulators, Luce Hall Planetarium, the Luce Hall Local Area Network and the electronic classrooms in Luce Hall. Summer training is required for all midshipmen and it is during this training that midshipmen get first-hand exposure to, and appreciation of, the duties, views, skills and abilities of enlisted men and women that midshipmen must later lead as officers. During summer training, midshipmen also learn to respect and handle the power of currents and wind aboard sailboats and in Yard Patrol (YP) craft.

Plebe Summer training starts on I-Day early in July and focuses on basic seamanship and sailing, military indoctrination, physical education, small arms training, and first-aid. During the summer between fourth-class and third-class year, midshipmen spend three weeks either on a 44 foot sloop or they spend three weeks at sea on a 108 foot YP on an 1,100 mile cruise up the New England seaboard. During a very intense and full summer between third-class year and second-class year, midshipmen become familiar with the operations of each branch of both the Navy and the Marine Corps. Midshipmen participate in a second-class cruise around the world on Navy ships and submarines for four weeks where they participate in drills, standing watches and gunnery exercises. Over an additional three week period called PROTRAMID (PROfessional TRAining of MIDshipmen), they participate in mock battles with the Marine Corps, they fly aboard Navy aircraft and dive in a nuclear submarine off of the coastal waters Florida. Finally, during the summer between second-class year and first-class year, midshipmen participate in four weeks with an operational unit of the Navy, either submarine, aircraft carrier, surface warship, aviation squadron, or special warfare unit. Midshipmen interested in the Marine Corps attend the Leatherneck course in Quantico, Virginia. Also, a large group of midshipmen serves in a leadership capacity, supporting the third-class YP summer deployment program, or training the newly reporting plebe class. A select group of midshipmen first-class may also participate in a foreign exchange cruise with an allied navy.

Finally, the Department of Sailing Programs is run out of the state-of-the-art Robert Crown Sailing Center on the Severn River. It provides an excellent opportunity for midshipmen to learn the secrets of the sea on Lasers, 40 and 60 foot ocean racers and 44 foot sloops. After Plebe Summer, sailing is voluntary and can be taken on an extracurricular level or a varsity level. The Sailing Program provides midshipmen with physical and tactical challenges while developing teamwork and leadership skills.

Military duty is not just a job, but a noble and patriotic calling which by its very nature includes sacrificing one's own needs, and possibly one's own life, to the greater common good of our nation. The Naval Academy has a comprehensive Professional Development Program, where midshipmen are thoroughly prepared for the military academically and in the practicalities of being an officer in the Navy or the Marine Corps. But the Academy goes beyond academics and practicalities, it emphasizes values such as integrity, respect, honor and "right" behavior. In this day and age of relativistic ethics and the "me first" attitude, the Naval Academy provides us all with a moral anchor as it indoctrinates its charges with both knowing and doing the right thing, even when nobody is watching. With its Honor Concept, Honor Treatise and Division of Character Development, the U.S. Naval Academy distinguishes itself as an educational institution that ennobles those who have chosen to serve.

SEA TRIALS - At the end of plebe year, the fourth-class participate in a group-test, known as Sea Trials, to determine both their teamwork abilities and readiness to become upperclassmen. This fourteen hour test of cooperative and team effort highlights the plebes' abilities to endure and work with others. Sea Trials is a "capstone" event for the fourth-class, similar to the Marine Corps' Crucible and the Navy's Battle Stations Program. Sea Trials also provides the upperclass with an opportunity to test and further develop their leadership capabilities.

SEA TRIALS - During Sea Trials, second-class midshipmen are responsible for plebe companies and third-class midshipmen are in charge of the plebe squads. They mentor and encourage the plebes throughout the event. In an effort to ensure that Sea Trials is safe, all midshipmen start training for the event months in advance. Part of the training is event specific, and part involves getting up at six in the morning to do runs in boots and utilities. The midshipmen even go through a "Mock Sea Trials" to get an idea of what to expect and to ensure that there are no logistical difficulties on the actual day of Sea Trials.

YARD PATROL CRAFT (YPs) - The Yard Patrol (YP) Craft is of wood-hull construction, diesel powered and accommodates twenty-four midshipmen, two instructors and four crew members. The YP was originally designed for midshipmen. They are used for training midshipmen in ship-handling, navigation, "Rules of the Road", fleet-tactical maneuvering principles and shipboard military procedures. YPs can cruise for up to five days or 1,400 nautical miles without having to refuel or restock, at a speed of twelve knots.

The Officer-in-Charge on the YP is a commissioned officer who has the responsibility for the safe passage of the ship and the training of the midshipmen. A YP crew consists of four enlisted personnel, a Craft Master (a senior Boatswains Mate or Quartermaster), an Engineman and two deck seamen. The Craft Master is responsible for ship safety, skillful navigation, and reliable communications with other vessels and shore stations. The enlisted lend their expertise in various areas, often giving briefs and control evolutions on the scene.

NAVIGATION SIMULATOR

NAVIGATION TRAINING - Midshipmen learn to navigate in darkness in a classroom simulator. From the navigation instruments to the nautical chart, midshipmen learn everything they need to know to successfully steer and maneuver a ship in a variety of situations.

NAVIGATION CLASSES

LEADERSHIP SPECIAL LECTURES

NAVIGATION CLASSES

LAW CLASSES

NAVIGATION TRAINING - In the classroom, midshipmen learn how to use navigational charts, digital navigation software and how to pilot and prepare for anchoring. Naval Academy graduates often come back to share their experiences and talk to midshipmen about such topics as leadership. A Judge Advocate General (JAG) officer speaks to midshipmen about legal regulations.

SURFACE SHIP TRAINING - Away from the walls of the Yard, midshipmen prepare for the fleet with hands-on experience aboard various vessels all over the world. Surface ships generally are built to fight other ships, submarines or aircraft, and can carry out several other missions including counter-narcotics operations and maritime interdiction. Their primary purpose is to engage space, air, surface, and submerged targets with weapons deployed from the ship itself.

SURFACE SHIP TRAINING - Midshipmen pull mooring lines aboard a ship during training. Midshipmen third-class are assigned a four week summer cruise aboard a naval vessel. While onboard, they become a part of the crew. They are assigned to a junior petty officer, and are assimilated into the ship's organization as they take part in gunnery exercises, damage control drills and standing watches. The midshipmen eat on the mess decks and sleep in crew berthing, participating in all of the daily activities alongside enlisted men and women.

SUBMARINE TRAINING

SUBMARINE TRAINING

SUBMARINE TRAINING

TRIDENT SUBMARINE

SUBMARINE TRAINING - Submarine training is done on classroom simulators and aboard actual submarines. Midshipmen learn much of what it takes to successfully serve aboard a submarine. In a room with leaky pipes, midshipmen learn the important job of fixing leaks that could occur aboard a submarine. All personnel must know every job so everything runs smoothly in the event that someone is unable to perform his or her job.

SUBMARINE TRAINING - Nuclear Attack Submarine off the coast of Florida. On a nuclear submarine, junior officers lead divisions of 10 to 20 men and women with responsibilities in a vital area of operations such as engineering, weapons or communications. They also stand watches and work to qualify as Engineering Officer of the Watch, Diving Officer and Officer of the Deck -- all steps towards earning the gold dolphins of a Navy submarine officer.

MARINE AMPHIBIOUS ASSAULT VEHICLE (AAV) TRAINING - Midshipmen receive training aboard AAVs, which are designed to assault any shoreline from the well decks of Navy assault ships. AAVs are highly mobile, tracked and armored amphibious vehicles that transport Marines and cargo to and through hostile territory.

MARINE TRAINING – CAMP LEJEUNE - As a part of Professional Development, midshipmen are exposed to various military environments that they might encounter during their careers. Midshipmen become familiar with warfare on tanks and other assault vehicles. They continue with rigorous physical training in the field and on camp-outs. All midshipmen must learn to take apart, put together and fire weapons with precision and accuracy.

MARINE TRAINING – THE MOUT - The Mout is short for Military Operations on Urban Terrain. This simulation of a small town teaches future Marine officers how to penetrate a town in a war zone. They are taught about the environment and what to expect. Their success in this training depends on their ability to determine who is and is not the enemy and to react accordingly.

MARINE TRAINING – THE MOUT - Midshipmen cover all angles as they approach the simulated town and are prepared to react quickly and accurately.

AMPHIBIOUS ASSAULT, LITTLE CREEK, VA - Seven-ton trucks are used to carry supplies to Marines on land. Amphibious Assault Ships are used to transport Marines and their equipment ashore. Landing craft are used to bring a landing force (infantry and vehicles) from ships to the shore during an amphibious assault. A hovercraft is capable of travelling over land, water, mud, ice and other surfaces. They can carry up to 75 tons of cargo and deliver loads directly onto beaches.

DUCK BOAT - Bringing Marines and supplies to shore. Excelling at approaching and crossing beaches in amphibious warfare attacks, these vehicles are used for the transportation of goods and troops over land and water.

BELL BOEING MV-22 OSPREY

BELL AH-1 COBRA ATTACK HELICOPTER

BELL AH-1 COBRA ATTACK HELICOPTER

SIKORSKY CH-53 STALLION HELICOPTER

MARINE CORPS AVIATION - The Osprey is a multi-mission, military aircraft with vertical takeoff and landing capabilities. It combines the functionality of a conventional helicopter with the long-range, high-speed cruise performance of a turboprop aircraft. The Bell AH-1 Cobra attack helicopter is multi-role combat helicopter. The CH-53 is a heavy-lift transport helicopter that can transport troops and heavy equipment.

SIKORSKY CH-53 STALLION HELICOPTER

MARINE CORPS AVIATION - The CH-53 features a six-bladed main rotor and four-bladed tail rotor. It holds
55 troops for transport and is armed with defensive countermeasures including an AN/ALE-39 chaff dispenser and
an AN/ALQ-157 infrared countermeasure.

NAVAL AVIATION - Navy and Marine Corps aviators are constantly called upon to perform under pressure. When assigned this career path, graduates can select training as a pilot or a naval flight officer. Pilots fly aircraft while naval flight officers serve as bombardiers, navigators, radar and electronic intercept officers and antisubmarine warfare systems specialists. Midshipmen train aboard prop planes, where they acquire mission critical aviation skills necessary to carry-out current and future missions.

NAVAL AVIATION - The FA-18 is a twin-engine carrier-capable multirole fighter aircraft. The U.S. Navy flies both the F/A-18E single-seater and F/A-18F two-seater in combat roles. The FA-18 Super Hornet is a twin-engine supersonic carrier capable aircraft that was built for air superiority.

NAVAL ACADEMY FOOTBALL - On weekends during the fall, the Naval Academy is consumed with the excitement of Navy football. The enthusiasm begins with the entire Brigade marching on to the field before the game. They stand shoulder to shoulder and snap a crisp salute to our National Anthem. That's what it's all about.

SPORTS

While the Naval Academy is committed to the moral, academic and professional development of its midshipmen, it is equally committed to their physical development. With one of the most comprehensive sports programs in the nation, the Naval Academy requires all midshipmen to participate in one of the three levels of sports: Varsity (Intercollegiate), Intramural or Club level. Naval Academy sports promote the development of qualities and values required of military officers: leadership, cooperation, teamwork, physical fitness and the ability to motivate others to excel. By competing in the athletic arena, midshipmen develop a winning attitude that will transcend into succeeding in combat.

Midshipmen compete against many of the best teams and individuals in college athletics all over the country. In conference play, the Naval Academy is aligned with similarly prestigious universities. Most Navy programs vie for championships in the Patriot League, while others contend with Ivy League institutions.

Navy teams have enjoyed success on the national landscape. Many teams have achieved regular and post season success and advanced to the NCAA Championships. The football team often appears in post-season bowl games. Many Naval Academy athletes have received some of our nation's most prestigious awards and have gone on to attain leadership roles. Rear Admiral Alan B. Shepard was the first man in space and a former heavyweight crew member. Ex-football lineman Admiral Stansfield Turner became director of the Central Intelligence Agency. Admiral Arleigh Burke, a former wrestler, later became Chief of Naval Operations. Rear Admiral Richard Bryd, the polar explorer, once captained the gymnastics team. Former Navy oarsman, Fleet Admiral Chester Nimitz, was commander of the Pacific Fleet during World War II and directed the U.S. victories at Midway, Iwo Jima and Okinawa. Fleet Admiral William "Bull" Halsey, former football player, commanded the task force on the carrier Enterprise in a series of raids against Japanese-held targets in World War II. Former football players Roger Staubach and Joe Bellino won the Heisman Trophy. David Robinson, who is widely considered to be the best basketball player in Naval Academy history, went on to play center for the San Antonio Spurs in the National Basketball Association.

Varsity Sports consist of 19 men's and 10 women's varsity teams. Men's Varsity Sports are baseball, basketball, heavyweight crew, lightweight crew, cross-country, football, golf, gymnastics, lacrosse, soccer, sprint football, squash, swimming & diving, tennis, indoor track, outdoor track, water polo and wrestling. Women's Varsity Sports consist of basketball, crew, cross country, golf, lacrosse, soccer, swimming & diving, tennis, indoor track, outdoor track and volleyball. Co-Ed Varsity Sports are rifle, intercollegiate sailing and offshore sailing.

Annapolis is the perfect location for Navy sailing. The Robert Crown Sailing Center, located on the Severn River, is the hub of all sailing activity at the Academy and is home of the Intercollegiate Sailing Hall of Fame. With one of the most active sailing programs in the nation, each year the Academy team sails in more than 60 college and one-design regattas during the fall and spring sailing seasons.

Intramural Sports teams practice and compete at the Company or Battalion level. In the fall, company teams compete in basketball, flag football, racquetball, soccer and ultimate frisbee. In the spring, teams compete in field ball, street hockey, soccer, ultimate frisbee and volleyball. Club Sports teams are not sanctioned by the NCAA, but they do compete against area colleges. Men's club sports include boxing, ice hockey, lacrosse, rugby and volleyball. Women's club sports include rugby and softball. Co-Ed club sports include cycling, fencing, judo, karate, marathon, pistol, powerlifting, and triathlon.

The Naval Academy has outstanding athletic facilities for intercollegiate and intramural sports, physical education and personal fitness, which symbolize its dedication to the development of its midshipmen. In addition to its newly renovated 34,000 seat Navy-Marine Corps Memorial Stadium, there is an 18-hole golf course, the newly renovated Max Bishop Baseball Stadium, the all-weather-surfaced Rip Miller Field for soccer, football and lacrosse and a synthetic-surfaced outdoor track. The new Wesley Brown Field House is a 140,000-square-foot facility for several sports activities and the 16,300-square-foot Glenn Warner Soccer Facility houses the men's and women's soccer teams. Lejeune Hall houses an Olympic-sized swimming pool with diving platforms, a wrestling area and conditioning areas. Alumni, Ricketts, Hubbard and MacDonough Halls also contain athletic facilities for several sports, and Halsey Field House, synthetic-surfaced throughout, includes a track, a climbing wall and a portable wooden basketball floor.

The Physical Education Department has specific requirements for each of a midshipman's four years at the Academy. Midshipmen are taught the basics of personal defense and lifelong habits in fitness and recreational sports. All midshipmen must pass the Physical Readiness Test regularly during their four years. All of the physical education requirements must be met in order for a midshipman to graduate.

Naval Academy graduates are well-prepared physically to meet the demands of being an officer in the Navy or Marine Corps. As a result of the Academy's dedication, midshipmen have both the facilities and the opportunity to experience a profound appreciation of physical fitness, teamwork and leadership.

THE BAND, THE CHEERLEADERS AND FOOTBALL – The Naval Academy Drum and Bugle Corps escorts midshipmen into the stadium, provides uplifting musical entertainment from the stands and marches in formation at half-time. By combining high energy entertainment with gymnastics and dance moves, the Navy Cheerleaders keep the spirits high during the game and compete on their own against other cheerleading squads. As a part of the American Athletic Conference, the Navy Football team faces opponents such as Houston, Memphis and Tulane; and also regularly plays against Air Force, Army, and Notre Dame.

As you watch the entire Brigade of Midshipmen march into The Navy-Marine Corps Stadium before each game, you wonder if there is an end to the companies of men and women coming into the stadium and lining up on the field. And finally, it ends with the Midshipmen getting the crowd excited with their own cheer or song and chanting, "Go Navy!"

United States Naval Academy game days in Annapolis are packed with entertainment – the Brigade of Midshipmen march from the Naval Academy through Annapolis to the stadium and take their places on the field for the opening ceremony. Every midshipman must attend every game. The midshipmen and the crowd are often entertained with flybys by fighter jets.

THE NAVY CHEERLEADERS take an active role in leading the Brigade's spirit at all Navy football games and all home men's and women's basketball games, pep rallies, pre-game "tailgates" and other spirit activities. **BILL THE GOAT** is the mascot of the United States Naval Academy athletic teams. He is a live goat and is also represented by a costumed midshipman. El Cid was the first goat mascot given to the Brigade by officers of the *USS New York* in 1893.

THE ARMY-NAVY GAME - is one of the most enduring rivalries in college football. At the writing of this book, Navy leads the all-time series with a record of 59 wins, 49 losses, and seven ties. A tradition for any sitting President attending the game, Former President George W. Bush crosses the field at half time to sit on the opposite side. He attended the Army-Navy Game three times during his Presidency. The week before the game is Spirit Week – a week full of pranks, pep rallies and other events where midshipmen show their Navy Spirit.

The Brigade of Midshipmen takes the field first if they are the "visiting" team and second if they are the "home" team. Since The Army-Navy game is played in various locations, the designation of home and visiting goes back and forth from year to year.

MEN'S VARSITY BASKETBALL - The U.S. Naval Academy began varsity intercollegiate competition in men's basketball in the 1907–08 season and has established itself as a force to be reckoned with. Known for its teamwork, Navy Men's Basketball dazzles its fans with a formidable showing each season.

Men's Varsity Basketball is played on the Basketball Court in Alumni Hall with seating for 5,710. Facing teams such as Army, Bucknell, Boston University and Colgate. Navy plays in the NCAA Division I and competes in the Patriot League.

WOMEN'S VARSITY BASKETBALL - For more than 30 years, the Women's Varsity Basketball team has set many records and won the Patriot League Championship in 2011. The team faces rival teams Army and Air Force, and other formidable opponents such as Lehigh, Lafayette, Harvard and Florida.

Women's Varsity Basketball is played on the Basketball Court in Alumni Hall. The team is ready to make its next move after it scores another basket.

MEN'S VARSITY BASEBALL - The baseball team plays its home games at the newly renovated, 3,000-seat Max Bishop Stadium. The team is a member of the Patriot League, which is part of the National Collegiate Athletic Association's Division I. The Naval Academy started playing baseball in the late 1860's and began playing other schools in 1893.

MEN'S HOCKEY - Navy Hockey made its debut on a pond in 1971. Since that time, Navy Hockey is played at the new athletic facility at Naval Support Activity Annapolis and competes at the American Collegiate Hockey Association Division 1 level in the Eastern Collegiate Hockey Association. A dedicated team, their five-month season includes thirty-plus games and on-ice practice five days a week. The players also invest a substantial amount of time in community programs and in Navy Youth Hockey.

MEN'S BOXING - The boxing program at the Naval Academy started in 1865, and today the Naval Academy's Brigade Boxing Championship generates hundreds of spectators and fans. Scoring is done under the official National Collegiate Boxing Association Boxing Rules, with points awarded for blocking and parrying, aggressiveness, attack and defense and generalship. The boxing team participates in invitational competitions in the fall and spring, as well as in ongoing intramural bouts. The Brigade Boxing Championship showcases the most elite midshipmen boxers, each performing in three-round matches within their weight class.

WRESTLING

SOCCER

RUGBY

KARATE - TAE KWON DO

WRESTLING - Wrestling at the Naval Academy began in 1920. The team competes at the Wesley A. Brown Field House for home meets and tournaments. **SOCCER** - The team began play in 1921 and competes as a member of the Patriot League. The team plays at the new Glenn Warner Soccer Facility. **RUGBY** - Founded in 1963, Navy Rugby is one of the most successful college rugby programs in the country. **KARATE** - The Naval Academy offers Judo and Karate as Club Sports and competes in the National Collegiate Karate Association and National Collegiate Judo Association.

VARSITY OUTDOOR TRACK & FIELD - Both men and women compete in outdoor track and field events. The Naval Academy's Men's Track and Field Team has been successful for years. The Navy Women's Track and Field Team was elevated to Division I status in 1991. Home events are held at Ingram Field.

VARSITY INDOOR TRACK & FIELD - Both men and women compete in indoor track and field events in the Wesley Brown Field House. The Men's and Women's teams are very competitive and have won several championship titles.

SWIMMING & DIVING - Men and women compete in swimming and diving events at the Varsity level. In 2011 Navy Men moved into the top 25 in NCAA Division I polling. The 2010-11 team handed Princeton its first ever loss in Denunzio Pool at Princeton, 167-133. The team also won its eighth straight Patriot League title and third straight Eastern College Athletic Conference title.

SWIMMING - Lejeune Hall, built in 1982, with an Olympic-sized pool, diving platforms and tank is the perfect atmosphere for swimming and diving at the Naval Academy.

NAVAL ACADEMY SAILING - Navy has one of our nation's most active sailing programs. Sailing at the Academy is both a requirement and a sport. During Plebe Summer, plebes have a total of 27 hours of sailing instruction aboard dinghies, keel boats and big boats. As a sport, Navy is host to more than fifteen dinghy regattas each year, partly because of its large fleet of boats. The noteworthy dinghy team has ample opportunity to practice as its fleet consists of 136 lasers, twenty-two 420's, 22 FJ's, two tech dinghies and four interclub dinghies.

The Naval Academy also hosts and competes in many intercollegiate big boat regattas. The Varsity Offshore Sailing Team has a fleet of Navy 44's, twelve J/24's and racing boats donated to the Naval Academy. The J/24's are used to give leadership opportunities to third-class midshipmen each fall, and are used to train the newest members of the offshore sailing team in the basics of sailing and teamwork.

NAVAL ACADEMY CREW - The crew teams are some of the Naval Academy's finest teams. Many men and women Navy oarsmen have represented the Academy and our country in Pan-American and Olympic games. Established in 1978, Women's Crew has produced several world-class athletes during its brief history. Heavyweight crew began more than 125 years ago with intramural crews racing in craft similar to whale boats.

As a crew team rows back to Hubbard Hall, two USNA buildings, Rickover and Nimitz Library stand out in the background. The state-of-the-art Fisher Rowing Center, one of the finest collegiate rowing facilities available in the country, is located in Hubbard Hall. It includes a ten-man indoor rowing tank with eight Fitron machines, a 3,500-square-foot weight room and a shell storage area that can accommodate 28, eight-oared boat shells. More than 200 crew athletes train there daily.

THE COLOR PARADE – The Brigade of Midshipmen are lined up on Worden Field for the Color Parade. This will be the last parade for graduating seniors. The yellow flags out in front of each company are called guidons. Since the times of the Roman Legions, the guidon has been a symbol of company's solidarity and pride.

COMMISSIONING WEEK

Commissioning Week is a week of celebration and concludes with the most anticipated ceremony of all – graduation and commissioning. Commissioning Week consists of formal dances, receptions, picnics, concerts, athletic events, parades, ceremonies and the Superintendent's garden parties. Friends, family and the general public are encouraged to attend many of these traditional celebrations.

During the first afternoon of Commissioning Week, all plebes participate in the Plebe Recognition Ceremony which punctuates the end of Plebe Year and marks the passage from plebe to upper class status. Cannons fire as plebes charge the Herndon monument and begin building a human ladder to climb the monument which has been covered with vegetable shortening by upper classmen. This event highlights the persistence and teamwork the Plebes have developed over the past year. Spectators and plebes all cheer and moan as progress to the top of the monument ebbs and flows. Tradition dictates that whoever reaches the top first and places his or her hat on top of the twenty-foot tall obelisk will be the first admiral from the class. Although this has not been proven true in the past, the Superintendent awards that person a set of Admiral's shoulder boards.

Among the notable social events of the week is the Ring Dance for the second-class midshipmen. During this formal affair, they receive their class rings. Prior to the dance, the midshipmen's dates place the class ring around their necks on a blue ribbon. Later, at the dance, the midshipmen's dates dip the rings in a binnacle containing waters from the Seven Seas, symbolizing the travels that lies ahead for the future naval officers. Afterward, the couples enter a huge replica of the ring where each date places the ring on the midshipman's finger and seals the ceremony with a kiss.

Thousands of visitors to the Academy enjoy the highlights of Commissioning Week. One of the most anticipated events is breath-taking air show performed by the Blue Angels. This demonstration of their precision and skill is a salute to the graduating class. This demonstration showcases choreographed naval aviation with graceful and precise maneuvers of six jets moving in unison, the famous six-jet Delta Formation.

The Color Parade is another anticipated highlight. Every year there is an intra-brigade competition to decide which of the 30 companies has the highest overall standing. Academics, sports, professional drills and parade performance are the deciding criteria. The Company accumulating the most points becomes the Color Company for the next academic year. During the Color Parade, the winning company is presented with a special guidon with a pennant bordered in blue. After the Color Parade, it is a tradition for the plebes to race to the pool and throw their Company Commanders in the pool, uniform and all, a fitting end to their duties as midshipmen. The Color Parade is the last parade in which the first-class midshipmen will participate at the Academy.

After a whirlwind of activities, Commissioning Week concludes with the first class preparing to participate in their last formal ceremony at the Naval Academy – Graduation. On the morning of graduation, family and friends assemble at Navy-Marine Corps Memorial Stadium with under-class midshipmen. An exciting and emotional day, graduation is the culmination of four memorable, rewarding and sometimes trying years. Among the honored main speakers is sometimes the President of the United States.

Once Bachelor of Science degrees are conferred by the Superintendent and the Academic Dean, the much anticipated oath of office is administered. The Commandant of the Marine Corps administers the oath to those who have chosen to be Marine Corps Officers and the Chief of Naval Operations administers the oath to those who have chosen the become Navy Officers. Afterward, the senior midshipman of the new first-class leads three cheers for "those about to leave us," and the newly commissioned officers, led by their class president, reply with three cheers for "those we leave behind." On the last "hooray" of this cheer, the graduates triumphantly toss their covers into the air, never having to wear them again. They are replaced with Navy and Marine Corps officers' covers that signify the end of one journey and the beginning of another.

MIDSHIPMEN'S HAT IS FINALLY PUT ON TOP

HERNDON MONUMENT CLIMB

1995 LONGEST HERNDON CLIMB

THE PLEBE RECOGNITION CEREMONY is an important ritual as the plebes become third-classmen or sophomores. They climb the Herndon Monument which has been covered with vegetable shortening by upperclassmen and change covers on top of the monument to show that they have conquered plebe year. The plebes work together as a team, as classmates are hoisted upon classmates until one reaches the top of the monument. The plebe hat is removed from the pinnacle and replaced by a midshipman's hat.

1995 LONGEST HERNDON CLIMB

The longest climb belongs to the class of 1998: During Commissioning Week in 1995, it took more than four hours to get the plebe hat off and put a midshipman's hat on the top. The courage, passion and hardship of the climb to the top characterize the struggle faced by the man for whom this monument is named. It was named after Commander William Lewis Herndon, who struggled valiantly to save the ship *Central America* and the men aboard it during a hurricane off of the coast of Savannah, Georgia in 1857. Commander Herndon perished with his ship.

COMPANY GUIDONS DISPLAYED AT COLOR PARADE

COLOR GUARD AT COLOR PARADE

COLOR PARADE

CHAPLAINS SAYING GOOD BYE AT COLOR PARADE

THE COLOR PARADE, established in 1867, is the Academy's oldest and most notable parade. The 30 companies compete for "top company" in a year-long competition involving teamwork, academics, athletics and professional abilities. At the end of the year, the winning company is given the honor of carrying the colors for the Brigade during the upcoming academic year. During Commissioning Week, just before graduation, the Color Company from the previous year transfers the colors to the new Color Company.

140

THE BLUE ANGELS - The Blue Angels is the United States Navy's flight demonstration squadron, with aviators from the Navy and Marines. The Blue Angels team, formed in 1946, is the second-oldest formal flying aerobatic team (under the same name) in the world. The Blue Angels' six demonstration pilots fly the F/A-18 Hornet.

MARINE CORPS OFFICERS TAKING OATH OF OFFICE

PRESIDENT OBAMA ADDRESSES MIDSHIPMEN

PRESIDENT OBAMA AND GOVERNOR O'MALLEY

NAVAL OFFICERS TAKE OATH OF OFFICE

GRADUATION - Held in the Navy-Marine Corps Stadium (or Alumni Hall if it rains), Graduation is the "main event" of Commissioning Week. Wearing the uniforms of the branch of service they have selected, midshipmen graduate and are commissioned as officers in the Navy or Marine Corps. The graduation speaker rotates every four years and includes the President, Vice President, the Chairman of the Joint Chiefs of Staff and Secretary of Defense.

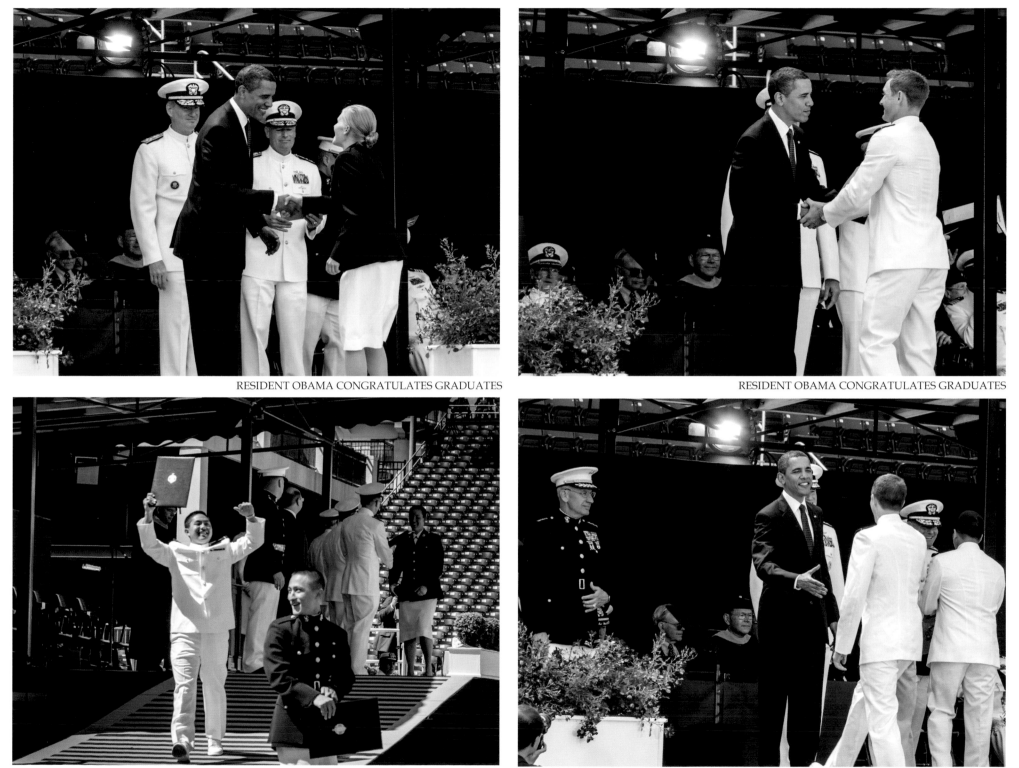

RESIDENT OBAMA CONGRATULATES GRADUATES

RESIDENT OBAMA CONGRATULATES GRADUATES

"AFTER FOUR YEARS, WE ARE FINISHED"

RESIDENT OBAMA CONGRATULATES GRADUATES

GRADUATES receive their diplomas from the Superintendent and the Academic Dean. President Obama offers a hearty handshake and congratulates them for their achievement. After the oath of office is administered and the diplomas are presented, the graduates sing "Navy Blue and Gold."

GOOD BYE TO COMPANY OFFICERS

MOM AND DAD PIN ON NEW OFFICER'S BARS

GOOD BYE TO COMPANY OFFICERS

CELEBRATING WITH FAMILY

GRADUATION The ceremony is only part of the formalities. It is also a time for saying good-bye to the officers, faculty, staff and classmates with whom these new graduates have developed close relationships over the last four years. Friends and family members are anxious to congratulate the new officers and participate in pinning on the new Navy ensign's shoulder-boards or the Marine Corps second lieutenant's gold bars.

HAT TOSS

HAT TOSS - The class president of the new first-class leads three cheers for "those who are about to leave us," and the new graduates, led by their class president, answer with three cheers for "those we leave behind." On the last cheer, all of the graduates toss their hats into the air, symbolizing the end of life as a midshipman. The Hat toss began in 1912. The midshipman's hat is replaced by an Ensign's or Second Lieutenant's hat..

SALUTE – When armed with a rifle, midshipmen will offer a "rifle salute." When armed with a drawn sword, they will salute with the sword. When in ranks, only the midshipman in charge will salute. A salute is a gesture of greeting and respect.

DISTINGUISHED NAVAL ACADEMY GRADUATES

The Naval Academy has a remarkable history of creating leaders of character who distinguish themselves from others in a variety of ways. In addition to military service that goes above and beyond the call of duty, Naval Academy graduates have excelled in areas such as national and international politics, sports, business and industry. The Naval Academy has produced many scholars and recipients of honors and awards.

The Distinguished Graduate Award Program (DGA) was initiated by Rear Admiral Ronald F. Marryott, USN (Retired), USNA Class of 1957, when he was president and CEO of the United States Naval Academy Alumni Association. Rear Admiral Robert McNitt, USN (Ret.), Class of 1938, helped develop the concept to its current structure. The Alumni Association's Board of Trustees approved the DGA proposal, and in May 1998, the selection committee met under the chairmanship of Admiral Carlisle Trost, USN (Ret.), Class of 1953 to determine the nominating process.

Distinguished Graduates are the embodiment of what the Naval Academy strives to achieve in its mission: "To develop midshipmen morally, mentally and physically and to imbue them with the highest ideals of duty, honor and loyalty in order to graduate leaders who are dedicated to a career of naval service and have potential for future development in mind and character to assume the highest responsibilities of command, citizenship and government."

The Distinguished Graduate Award is presented from the United States Naval Academy Alumni Association to living graduates of the United States Naval Academy because of their demonstrated and unselfish commitment to a lifetime of service to our nation; personal character which epitomizes the traits expected of an officer; significant contributions as Navy and Marine Corps officers or as leaders in industry or government.

Admiral Thomas H. Moorer, USN (Retired), USNA Class of 1933, received the first award in 1999. Since then, awards have been given to more than 70 additional Distinguished Graduates. Recent distinguished graduates include: Rear Admiral Robert Shumaker, USN (Ret.), Class of 1956; Dr. Bradford Parkinson, Class of 1957; Lieutenant General Mathew Cooper, USMC (Ret.), Class of 1958; Mr. Corbin McNeill, Class of 1962; Admiral Sylvester R. Foley Jr., USN (Ret.), Class of 1950; The Honorable Daniel L. Cooper, Class of 1957; Captain Bruce McCandless II, USN (Ret.), Class of 1958; Vice Admiral John Ryan, USN (Ret.), Class of 1967; Mr. Daniel Akerson, Class of 1970; Mr. Roger E. Tetrault, Class of 1963; The Honorable J. Scott Redd, Class of 1966; Ambassador Richard L. Armitage, Class of 1967; Admiral Thomas B. Fargo, USN (Ret.), Class of 1970; Lieutenant General Thomas P. Stafford, USAF (Ret.), Class of 1952; Rear Admiral William C. Miller, USN (Ret.), Class of 1962; Admiral Charles S. Abbot, USN (Ret.), Class of 1966; Admiral Michael G. Mullen, USN (Ret.), Class of 1968; Admiral Edmund P. Giambastiani, Jr., USN (Ret.), Class of 1970; Admiral Henry H. Mauz, Jr., USN (Ret.), Class of 1959; Admiral Richard W. Mies, USN (Ret.), Class of 1967; Admiral James O. Ellis, Jr., USN (Ret.), Class of 1969 and Mr. David M. Robinson, Class of 1987.

The Distinguished Graduates serve as an example for our midshipmen as they begin to chart their naval careers and motivates alumni serving in the Navy and Marine Corps.

Nominations for this annual award are normally provided by the presidents of Alumni Association chapters or graduated classes. However, nominees need not necessarily be a member of the Chapter or Class presenting the nomination. A narrative detailing the nominee's contributions and distinguished service justifying his or her selection as the recipient of the Distinguished Graduate Award must accompany the nomination. Distinguished Graduates accept their awards at the Naval Academy.

The pages that follow provide four excellent examples of distinguished graduates and their reminiscences of their Naval Academy training and what it meant to their careers, accomplishments and personal lives: Rear Admiral William Miller, USN (Ret), Class of 1962; Captain Roger Tetrault, USNR (Ret), Class of 1963; Mr. Daniel Akerson, Class of 1970 and GEN Peter Pace, US Marine Corps (RET), Class of 1967.

Rear Admiral William C. Miller, '62, USN (Ret.)

I came to Annapolis as a 17-year-old from a small high school in Burbank, California. Before the day I was sworn in as a midshipman, I had never visited the Naval Academy, and had never even travelled east of the Mississippi River. I flew to Maryland alone that day; my parents couldn't afford to come with me. I was truly starting a new life, a new adventure, on my own.

Throughout my life the Naval Academy has provided a strong anchor to windward for me, a welcoming home away from home. I have been privileged to spend 19 years, more than a quarter of my life, living on the Academy grounds: 4 as a midshipman, 3 as a junior officer teaching and assisting in the Academy's administration, and later 12 as the Academic Dean and Provost, the Academy's civilian chief academic officer. Few other graduates have been so fortunate.

Not surprisingly, the Academy also has played an important role in my family's life. All of our five children have lived on the Yard, our youngest daughter was born on the Yard and baptized in the Academy Chapel, our oldest son graduated from the Academy (USNA '88) and married his bride in the Chapel, our oldest daughter married a graduate (USNA '76) in the Chapel, our youngest daughter was married in the Chapel, our oldest grandson is a USNA graduate (USNA '08), and as this is being written one of our granddaughters is a current midshipman (USNA '18). I had been the first in my family to attend the Naval Academy, but the Naval Academy has become an important part of the extended Miller household.

Many graduates probably look back at their time in the Navy or Marine Corps and conclude that the Academy gave them a jump start on their military careers – not a guarantee of success or a path to more rapid promotion than their contemporaries from civilian backgrounds; but the Naval Academy provided a firm foundation on which a graduate can build a successful military career if he or she is willing to put forth the effort. In looking back on my own military career, I share this conclusion; and recognize also how much the Academy helped me in my civilian career as well. As I transitioned from command in the military to an appointment as an engineering professor and academic leader in a civilian university, I was pleasantly surprised to find that the leadership skills and principles of personal integrity and mutual respect I learned in the military were welcomed in academia as well.

Finally, I will always be grateful to then-Naval Academy Superintendent Admiral Charles A. (Chuck) Larson for giving me the opportunity to tie my naval career to my civilian education career when he hired me as the Academy's Academic Dean and Provost. That assignment gave me the opportunity to give back to the Academy, to "pay it forward" in a sense by helping successive graduates to lay their own personal and professional foundations in Annapolis, as I had done more than five decades earlier.

Rear Admiral Bill Miller, former Naval Academy Academic Dean and Provost (1997-2009), contributed significantly to the Naval Academy's transition to the 21st Century. His Navy career included tours as a commanding officer on ships in the Atlantic and Pacific fleets. Ashore, he commanded the Naval Research Laboratory and Office of Naval Research. As a civilian, he served as Associate Provost and Professor of Engineering at West Virginia University before being selected as Dean and Provost at the Naval Academy.

Captain Roger E. Tetrault '63 USNR (Ret.)

Acceptance to the . Naval Academy was the ultimate game changer in my life. Coming from a very large lower-middle-class family, where neither parent had been educated beyond 7th grade, there was little or no expectation that we would go to college. Yet, I dreamed large and applied to the Naval Academy, hoping that I might get accepted.

Those dreams were realized when I received a telegram confirming my acceptance into the class of 1963. I received that telegram on May 29th, 1959. Given the very late date of this telegram, it is very possible that I was the last person accepted into the Class of 1963.

Upon entry, we were required to pay $600 for our initial uniform allowance. My parents did not have the required $600, nor did they have the ability to raise the money. The local Elks club, in my hometown of Huntington, N.Y., provided the $600 from their scholarship fund. In 1998, my wife and I were able to repay this enormous debt to the Huntington Elks club by endowing their scholarship program.

My civilian career began at a commercial facility that made nuclear reactors for Navy ships, where I started as a junior engineer. Ultimately, with many stops along the way, I became the Chief Executive Officer (CEO) and Chairman of the Board of one of our nation's largest corporations, with significant operations around the world.

During my civilian career I was, at various times, in charge of the construction of such diverse high technology items as nuclear reactors, nuclear submarines, main battle tanks, electric power generation plants, deepwater off-shore oil platforms, and numerous others high technology products and services. In these various positions, my technical skills were tested every day. Thankfully, the education that I received at the Naval Academy was excellent preparation for operating in this high technology world.

After retiring from industry, I was asked by the NASA Administrator to serve on a task force to evaluate the management and cost projections for the International Space Station (ISS) construction program. This was followed by multiple appointments to the NASA Advisory Council (NAC).

In 2003, the space shuttle Columbia was lost on reentry from space. I was one of the 12 Board members charged with the investigation of this accident. Finally in 2005, I was assigned to a National Research Council Committee that would assess the options for extending the life of the Hubble telescope. Based on our recommendations, the Hubble Space Telescope was repaired in space by the astronauts of Flight STS-125.

The Naval Academy is very small by the number of graduates it produces, but it stands tall when it comes to impact. Year after year it out punches our country's much larger colleges and universities by producing a cadre of highly successful leaders, with an amazing diversity of occupational choices. Whether you look into the world of politics, law, medicine, business, or even the ministry, you are sure to find at least a few Naval Academy graduates that have substantial leadership roles. The Naval Academy produces "Leaders to serve the Nation." That challenge is fulfilled every day by its graduates, who through their honesty, integrity, commitment, and intelligence stand as living proof that a Naval Academy education is among the best anywhere in the world

Captain Roger E. Tetrault graduated in 1963, earned his wings in 1966, served two tours of duty in Vietnam aboard "Turner Joy," joined the Navy Reserve in 1970, retired as a captain in 1985, was the Chairmen of the Board and CEO of McDermott International, President of General Dynamics' Electric Boat Division, NASA Committee reviewing International Space Station, NASA Hubble Space Telescope, NASA Advisory Council and Columbia Accident Investigation Board, awarded the NASA Distinguished Public Service Medal.

Daniel "Dan" Akerson '70

Like many of my classmates, I came of age in small-town America and within days of my high school graduation, I left home for the first time to head for the Academy to become a midshipman. Sounds exciting, but the details are a little less colorful.

Flying for the first time in my life, I arrived at Washington National Airport and then took the Greyhound bus to Annapolis. I had to lug my fully loaded suitcase from the West Street Station to Gate One, where reality set in. The Marine guard informed me that I was a day early and that I might try finding a room in one of the drag houses along Prince George Street. Fortunately, an understanding woman took me in and let me sleep on a rug in her entryway, providing a pillow and blanket, bathroom down the hall, for $5.

The Academy was a little less nurturing then than it is today. As plebes, our new reality was summed up at the swearing in ceremony, when we were told: "Look to your left, now look to your right. One of you won't be here in 4 years."

The late 60s were a time of great change and turmoil in America. The Vietnam War was raging, the space race was in full tilt, race relations were not good, the women's rights movement was emerging, and the drug culture was taking hold. It wasn't all bad; we landed on the moon, Apollo 13 was miraculously saved by the tenacity and ingenuity of its crew (led by USNA grad Jim Lovell), and the Mets won the World Series! In the midst of all this societal upheaval, I was drawn to the structure, discipline and purpose that the Naval Academy offered. To this day, I can recall the tenets of our mission that resonated then as they do today: "to develop midshipmen, morally, mentally and physically, in order to assume the highest positions of command, citizenship and government."

After graduation, I became a surface warfare officer in what was called, "the Mod Squad," serving on the destroyer, *USS DUPONT*. The ship and crew were awarded the Marjorie Sterrett Battleship Award. I concluded my naval service as head of the Naval Communications School in Norfolk, Virginia. Thereupon I resigned my commission and embarked on a civilian career that was diverse, exciting and with challenges I could not have imagined. The bedrock foundation and the fundamentals of leadership that I learned at the Academy and in the Navy served me well: competence, integrity, passion, accountability and decisiveness.

I've worked hard at every job I've had, often taking the high risk/high reward job with companies considered unlikely to succeed. I also completed a Master of Science (Economics) at the London School of Economics. With these educational credentials, I was drawn to companies at defining points in their histories: Phillips Petroleum's development of the first oil fields in the North Sea, MCI's successful assault on the AT&T monopoly, General Instrument's development and deployment of digital HD television, Nextel and The Carlyle Group. My greatest challenge came later in my career when, in the summer of 2009, the Obama Administration asked me to join the board of directors of the new General Motors Company. A year later, I was asked to become CEO and eventually chairman. It was a call to serve and I harkened back to our mission at the USNA: to assume the highest position of command, citizenship and government.

Not unlike midshipmen of today, I was afforded a wonderful education and the opportunity to serve our nation in many different ways. My only advice to this generation of young people would be: lean in and pay it forward, embrace life's challenges and do not fear failure. Remember, in the words of John Paul Jones "….he who will not risk, cannot win."

General Peter Pace, '67- US Marine Corps (Ret.)
16th Chairman of the Joint Chiefs of Staff

I set my sights on the U.S. Naval Academy at a very young age. After attending an Army-Navy Game as a child, I was enthralled with the precision of the "march on" and the energy of the competition – and I wanted to be a part of it all! But the path from my home in Teaneck, NJ to Bancroft Hall was not a direct one.

After failing the physical – 20/40 vision – I was admitted on a waiver, with the endorsement of the Academy's soccer coach. My soccer skills aside, the coach's example of investing in me - taking a risk on my behalf – planted a seed in my heart for those who might need a waiver to chase their dreams.

I entered the Academy with the vision of serving in submarines, majoring in nuclear engineering and completing a nuclear academic track. However, the summer opportunities provided a wide range of military service experiences, which helped me understand that the Marine Corps was a better fit for me. I wasn't sure if I could be a good Marine, but I wanted to try. I wanted to emulate what I saw in the Marine officers who were part of the Naval Academy cadre. I fully understood that my country was at war, and felt the best way I could serve would be on the ground, leading Marines in combat.

I was mentored by the best, and this example of guiding and developing others was a key element to my professional education. Rear Admiral Draper Kauffman was the Superintendent at the time, and the way he reached out to and brought us mids into his family was something I tried to emulate through out my career.

The Naval Academy experience made me realize that I could push myself physically and mentally beyond any previous definition of my limits. Academically, this recognition of working at something to my full potential did not materialize until far too late in my time at the Academy. I graduated with the feeling that I hadn't applied myself as well, or performed as well as I should have. I used this perspective to inspire me to give the Marine Corps my very best effort – and that has made all of the difference.

Over the next 40 years on active duty, I tried to apply these basic lessons on the importance of working hard, seeking out solid mentors while mentoring others, and taking care of those in my charge.

Another lesson I learned at the Academy is something I came to think of as the appreciation of five minutes. My most challenging assignments required more than making good decisions – but making good decisions under pressure of very short deadlines, with limited and sometimes conflicting information, in an uncomfortable and fluid environment, with significant consequences. The Academy taught me to deal with uncertainty by leaning out over my comfort level, coming up to speed quickly in unfamiliar situations, accepting reasonable risk, making decisions, and taking action on those decisions - all in the span of just a few minutes. With practice, this became an invaluable skill set that I applied at every assignment and post-retirement position.

The United States Naval Academy is not for everybody. It requires great focus, determination, and a deep desire to succeed. More than an education, it combines academics, sports, professional development, leadership, self-discipline, and introspection. The whole process was exactly right for me!

Born in Brooklyn and raised in Teaneck, NJ, General Peter Pace graduated from the Naval Academy and was commissioned a second lieutenant in the Marine Corps in June 1967. His career spanned more than 40 years of active service, beginning as a Rifle Platoon Leader in Vietnam and rising to serve as Vice Chairman (2001-2005) and then as Chairman of the Joint Chiefs of Staff (2005-2007). He holds the distinction of being the first Marine to have served in either of these positions. He earned a Master's Degree from George Washington University, attended Harvard University Senior Executives in National and International Security program, and graduated from the National War Collage. In 2008, General Pace was awarded the Presidential Medal of Freedom, the highest civilian honor a President can bestow. General Pace serves on the Board of several corporate entities, many involved in cyber security. He is a visiting professor for Fordham University, and frequent speaker at military and executive conferences. He and his wife Lynne are associated with a number of charities focused on supporting the troops and their families.

NAVAL ACADEMY ALUMNI ASSOCIATION - The Alumni Association began in 1886 when Lieutenant Commander Charles Belknap got together with 12 officers and started the association. It has continued to grow and now consists of all Alumni, Associate Members and parents of midshipmen. The Alumni Association has its own magazine, *Shipmate*, that supports its numerous events during the year and provides for the exchange of personal and class news among alumni.

MCMULLEN HOCKEY ARENA

ALUMNI HALL

NAVY-MARINE CORPS MEMORIAL STADIUM

WESLEY BROWN FIELD HOUSE

NAVAL ACADEMY FOUNDATION - The Foundation has supported the Naval Academy by raising, managing and distributing private gift funds. These private funds have created new buildings, sports facilities, scholarships and other assistance to support the mission of the Naval Academy.

Fireworks light the Annapolis sky. Annapolis is host to many celebrations and festivals throughout the year. Fireworks are often the finale of historic celebrations such as the Fourth of July or part of the "First Night" celebration on New Year's Eve. The event includes live musical entertainment and features two fireworks displays, an early show for families and early-risers and a traditional midnight spectacular to ring in the new year.

ANNAPOLIS

Annapolis, capital of Maryland, is one of our nation's most picturesque cities. Located midway between Washington, D.C. and Baltimore, Maryland, it is ideally situated as a port on the Chesapeake Bay.

Founded in 1649 by Puritans seeking religious freedom, it was originally located on the north shore of the Severn River and western shore of the Chesapeake Bay, across from its present location adjacent to the Naval Academy. The remainder of the century saw waterfront development on the banks of the creeks in the present "City Dock" area. It became known as Anne Arundel Town and was a principle colonial port suited for the export of tobacco, which was the backbone of the colony's economy.

In 1694, Governor Francis Nicholson proclaimed the village as the capital of Maryland because it was more centrally located – geographically and politically – than the colony's first capital, St. Mary's City. He renamed the town Annapolis, after James II's daughter, Princess Anne who later became Queen of England.

Annapolis was designed around two stately circles. The construction of Maryland's first State House began at the center of State Circle, not far from the harbor. It was completed in 1697. Just to the west, early planners laid out Church Circle as home to the Church of England. In 1708, Annapolis received a royal charter of incorporation.

Annapolis flourished from the mid-1700s until the American Revolution. Thomas Jefferson enjoyed strolling along the narrow old brick sidewalks around the Annapolis Harbor and George Washington also frequented and loved Annapolis. General Washington played horses at the race track just outside the city on what is now West Street. Annapolis was the site of the first parochial libraries and King William's School (now St. John's College). In spite of their close ties to London, Annapolitans supported the Revolution. The passage of the Stamp Act in 1765 stirred the first patriotic tempers, and an angry mob ran a tax collector out of town. On October 15, 1774, the brigantine, *Peggy Stewart* dropped anchor in the harbor carrying a load of highly-taxed English Tea. Ship-owner Anthony Stewart sailed the doomed boat a bit further upriver and torched it. Annapolis had its own Tea Party.

There were no large battles in Maryland during the Revolution. However, many troops passed through Annapolis. Among the most prominent wartime visitors was The Marquis de Lafayette, who bivouacked in Annapolis on his way to Yorktown in 1781. Congress met briefly in the State House on December 23, 1783 when General George Washington resigned his commission as commander-in-chief of the Continental Army. Weeks later, the Treaty of Paris was ratified, formally ending the war with Great Britain. For a short time, between November 1783 and August 1784, Annapolis served as the Capital of the United States.

The founding of the United States Naval Academy in 1845 spurred growth. The need for hotel rooms, taverns and restaurants resulted in a boom in the hospitality trade. Navy Frigates, including the USS Constitution, were stationed here for midshipmen training. A host of small sailboats drifted across the harbor daily as crews learned to sail. Patriotic fervor was stirred whenever sailors were sent to defend our country during a war.

Downtown Annapolis is a registered National Historic Landmark with more than 60 structures dating back to the 18th Century. Homes of Georgian and Colonial architecture such as the William Paca House, the Hammond-Harwood House and the Chase-Lloyd House grace its streets in close proximity to the Naval Academy.

Some of the main streets of Annapolis are reminiscent of colonial times in both name and appearance: Duke of Gloucester Street, King George Street, Prince George Street and Hanover Street. The State House, built during the 1770's, is the oldest state capitol still in use. The Shiplap Museum is one of the oldest houses in Annapolis and was formerly a tavern for colonial Americans. The oldest public building in Maryland, the Old Treasury Building, was built between 1735 and 1736 with thick brick walls, a mammoth wooden door and barred windows to protect the currency.

Annapolis visitors participate in an intimate relationship with Colonial America and have an infinite number of more contemporary and interesting things to also see and do. There are numerous art galleries, museums, theaters and tours of the city. Many visitors enjoy boating, swimming, fishing, crabbing, golfing and other sports. Annapolis offers dining experiences to suit every palate, historic inns and modern hotels. The town also offers wine tastings, a number of fun festivals and local pubs that feature jazz and modern music for entertainment. Annapolis has a rich sailing tradition dating back to colonial times. Known as Maryland's Sailing Capital, Annapolis is host to annual sailboat and powerboat shows and breathtaking weekly sailboat races.

As the capital of Maryland, Annapolis is host to the lawmakers who come to the State Senate and House from January to April every year. Their chambers have grown and become modernized, but the issues are basically the same – taxes, road construction, schools, fisheries and the safety of the population.

MARYLAND STATE HOUSE

MAIN STREET

HOUSE OF DELEGATES

GOVERNMENT HOUSE- GOVERNOR'S MANSION

THE MARYLAND STATE HOUSE dome rises above the trees with the American Flag flying on top against the blue sky. THE GOVERNOR'S MANSION/GOVERNMENT HOUSE has been the official residence of Maryland Governors since 1870. THE MARYLAND HOUSE OF DELEGATES is in session with its 141 members. MAIN STREET turns into a magical place to eat and shop when the lights come on and the evening begins.

AERIAL VIEW OF ANNAPOLIS – The historic district is in the foreground with Eastport across Spa Creek in the background to the right. At the center is the Maryland State House with the Governor's Mansion in front and to the right. Behind the State House, Main Street slants to the left and runs all the way to "Ego Alley" and Spa Creek. The Naval Academy is top left at the mouth of Spa Creek

PACA HOUSE AND GARDEN

THE PACA HOUSE AND GARDEN -This Georgian mansion was built in the 1760s by William Paca, one of Maryland's four Signers of the Declaration of Independence and the state's third Governor. Saved from destruction and restored over the last 50 years by Historic Annapolis, Inc., today this National Historic Landmark is recognized as one of the finest 18th-Century homes in the country and is open for public tours. The site's two-acre garden is a picturesque retreat from the bustle of the city. Visitors can view native and heirloom plants while exploring the terraced landscapes and formal Parterres.

PACA HOUSE DINNING ROOM

BRICE HOUSE

PACA HOUSE AND GARDEN

HOGSHEAD

THE JAMES BRICE HOUSE - It is one of the largest and most elegant historic Annapolis mansions. Construction started in 1767. Six years, 326,000 bricks and 90,800 cypress shingles later, it was completed. The House is now headquarters to the non-profit Historic Annapolis, Inc. **THE HOGSHEAD** - At the Hogshead, visitors learn what life was like for the early Maryland middle class with interactive experiences led by guides dressed in colonial attire. Be sure to see Scout Williams, also known as "Speedy" when you visit. The name Hogshead comes from the 18th Century 63 gallon barrel used to transport alcoholic beverages or a 48 inch tall by 30 inch wide unit used in transporting tobacco, the most valuable colonial crop.

It has been said that Annapolis is a "drinking" town with a "sailing problem." Annapolis, for many residents, is all about sailing. Weekends for them is all about sail boat races at the Annapolis Yacht Club or the Eastport Yacht Club.

Annapolis is uniquely located where sailing conditions are almost perfect. It is not too cold in the winter and not too hot in the summer. Both the wind and tides are mild and fairly consistent. The Chesapeake Bay provides protection from dangerous shorelines and offers smoother sailing than the ocean.

The custom of having a Color Guard was established in 1867 when the first Color Parade was held. Only two flags were carried in parades at that time, the national colors and the Navy infantry flag, consisting of a large blue field with a central, white diamond containing an anchor. Today, the Color Guard has a rifleman on each end and carries four flags: the national colors and the flags of the Department of the Navy, the U.S. Marine Corps, and the U.S. Naval Academy.

DIRECTORY OF PARTICIPANTS

UNITED STATES NAVAL ACADEMY
PUBLIC AFFAIRS OFFICE
U.S. Naval Academy
121 Blake Road
Annapolis, MD 21402
Tel: 410-293-1520
Tel: 410-293-2292 Media Requests
www.usna.edu

UNITED STATES NAVAL ACADEMY
U.S. NAVAL ACADEMY ADMISSIONS
U.S. Naval Academy
Armel-Lefteich Visitors Center
152 King George Street
2nd Deck
Annapolis, MD 21402
Tel: 410-293-1858
www.usna.edu

UNITED STATES NAVAL ACADEMY
U.S. NAVAL ACADEMY VISITORS CENTER
U.S. NAVAL ACADEMY GIFT SHOP
U.S. Naval Academy
Armel-Lefteich Visitors Center
152 King George Street
Annapolis, MD 21402
Tel: 410-263-4448 Tour Services
Tel: 800-778-4260 Gift Shop
www.navyonline.com

UNITED STATES NAVAL ACADEMY
U.S. NAVAL ACADEMY MUSEUM
U.S. Naval Academy
Preble Hall
118 Maryland Avenue
Annapolis, MD 21402
Tel: 410-293-2108
www.usna.edu/Museum

UNITED STATES NAVAL ACADEMY
NAVAL ACADEMY CHAPEL
U.S. Naval Academy
121 Blake Road
Annapolis, MD 21402
Tel: 410-293-1101 General
Tel: 410-293-1105 Wedding Coordinator

UNITED STATES NAVAL ACADEMY
NAVAL ACADEMY ATHLETIC
   ASSOCIATION
U.S. Naval Academy
Ricketts Hall
566 Brownson Road
Annapolis, MD 21402
Tel: 410-293-2700
Tel: 800-874-6289 Tickets
www.NavySports.com

UNITED STATES NAVAL ACADEMY
ALUMNI ASSOCIATION
247 King George Street
Annapolis, MD 21402
Tel: 410-295-4000
www.usna.com

UNITED STATES NAVAL ACADEMY
FOUNDATION
247 King George street
Annapolis, MD 21402
Tel: 410-295-4000
www.usna.com

BRIGADE SPORTS COMPLEX
64 Greenbury Point Road
Annapolis, MD 21402
Tel: 410-293-9700
McMullen Arena
Rankin Golf Center

THE CARTER CENTER
Office of Public Relations
One Copenhill
453 Freedom Parkway
Atlanta, Georgia 30307
Tel: 404-420-5117
www.cartercenter.org

PACA HOUSE AND GARDEN
Historic Annapolis, Inc.
186 Prince George Street
Annapolis, MD 21401
Tel: 410-267-7619
Tel: 410-990-4538 Wedding Coordinator

www.annapolis.org

HOGSHEAD
Historic Annapolis, Inc.
43 Pinkney Street
Annapolis, MD 21401
Tel: 410-267-7619
www.annapolis.org

SHIPLAP HOUSE
Historic Annapolis, Inc.
18 Pinkney Street
Annapolis, MD 21401
Tel: 410-267-7619
www.annapolis.org

BRICE HOUSE
Historic Annapolis, Inc.
42 East Street
Annapolis, MD 21401
Tel: 410-267-7619
www.annapolis.org

HISTORIC ANNAPOLIS MUSEUM STORE
Historic Annapolis, Inc.
99 Main Street
Annapolis, MD 21401
Tel: 410-267-6656
www.annapolis.org

HAMMOND-HARWOOD HOUSE
19 Maryland Avenue
Annapolis, MD 21401
Tel: 410-263-4683
www.harmmondharwoodhouse.org

CHASE-LLOYD HOUSE
22 Maryland Avenue
Annapolis, MD 21401
Tel: 410-263-2723
Open March-December 2 pm - 4 pm

STAINED-GLASS WINDOW AT THE NAVAL ACADEMY CHAPEL - This is one of four stained-glass windows along the right side of the chapel. The windows along the right depict verses from the Old Testament of the Bible. The four windows along the left side depict verses from the New Testament. This window, "God Cares for Man at Sea," features a ship in a storm with a hint of a rainbow, King David observing the landing of a ship and a ship on a calm night. At the bottom of the window is Psalm 107, verse 23.